MW00352051

Lawyers for the
Creative Arts

LCA *Law Guide*

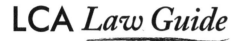

Band Law for Bands

Barry Irwin
Adam Reis

Editor: Jason Koransky

Second Edition

LAWYERS FOR THE CREATIVE ARTS

CHICAGO, ILLINOIS

The materials contained in this book represent the opinions and views of the authors and/or the editors, and should not be considered the opinions or views of the law firms with which the authors and/or editors are associated.

Nothing in this book should be considered as providing legal advice for a specific case, and readers of this book should obtain such legal advice from their own counsel. This book is intended for educational and informational purposes.

Book Designer: Patricia Rios
Cover Designer: Kristen Onesti

Library of Congress Cataloging-in-Publication Data
Irwin, Barry
Reis, Adam
Band Law for Bands
Barry Irwin & Adam Reis
Library of Congress Cataloging in-Publication Data is on File.

ISBN-13: 978-0-692-65090-5

ISBN-10: 0-692- 65090-5

To order copies of this book, please contact:

Lawyers for the Creative Arts:
213 Institute Place, Suite 403
Chicago, IL 60610
(312) 649-4111
info@law-arts.org

www.law-arts.org

Table of Contents

Chapter

Foreword to the Second Edition

In 2012, LCA decided to celebrate its 40th year of service to the arts by producing a series of books on arts-related legal topics. The goal was to explain basic legal principles in a way that would be accessible to practicing artists – in other words, individuals without law degrees. And so the *LCA Law Guide* series was born.

The *LCA Law Guide* is now three-volumes, with another forthcoming. The present volume is our first "second edition," incorporating many changes, updates and expansions from the first edition. This second edition is authored by the first edition co-author, Barry Irwin, with Adam Reis. Special thanks to Jason Koransky, who co-authored the first edition of *Band Law for Bands*, and who has been the Editor of the entire *LCA Law Guide* series since its inception.

This second edition of *Band Law for Bands* will be helpful to musicians of all kinds in learning the basic legal principles that apply in this area of law. We at Lawyers for the Creative Arts welcome your feedback!

Carol Anne Been
President, Board of Directors
Lawyers for the Creative Arts

About Lawyers for the Creative Arts

Since its founding in 1972, Lawyers for the Creative Arts has been the "go to" resource for legal advice crucial to the creative arts. Regardless of a client's ability to pay legal fees, LCA provides legal advice to individuals and organizations in the arts and entertainment communities directly and through our network of volunteer attorneys.

LCA serves individuals and organizations in all areas of the arts and entertainment, including the literary, visual, and performing arts. From string quartets to rock bands; from screenwriters to documentary filmmakers; from sketch artists to photographers; from stage actors to producers; from bronze casters to painters; from literary publishers to media houses; from museums to digital archivists; LCA helps them all navigate the complex legal system.

We have helped clients start businesses, draft contracts, and protect innovative designs and creations of every nature in every conceivable discipline of the arts. We help artists in litigation matters and we are equally active in helping to resolve claims out of court. Our Patricia Felch Arts Mediation Service exists to help artists resolve disputes quickly, privately, and outside the costly realm of courtroom litigation. Our popular nonprofit workshops are directed to artists seeking to organize as tax exempt corporations under state and federal law. We have helped thousands of organizations, including many of the most prominent and successful arts institutions in the area.

LCA operates with a small full-time staff, but we are backed up by hundreds of active private attorneys from the best firms in the area. Our volunteer lawyers are the true heroes who level the playing field when clients are at a disadvantage. They are willing to step up and contribute their time and valuable expertise to our many thankful clients. They get it—that art, in all its forms, is an important and worthwhile piece of American culture, and that art and those who create it should have legal protection.

The long list of volunteer attorneys, together with LCA's dedicated staff, Board of Directors, Honors Council, and Associate Board, are the soul of LCA. With their support, artists are free to do what it is they do—bring color, texture, and wondrous sights and sounds to all of our lives.

Education is another key element of LCA. LCA provides materials, conducts workshops, and gives seminars on not-for-profit incorporation and tax exemption, the law of music, publishing, film, copyright, and more. LCA gives presentations to dozens of schools, colleges, law groups, and arts groups each year. And, it mentors hundreds of young lawyers.

As LCA celebrates 44 years of service, we pledge to continue, with the help of the legal community and other supporters of the arts, to provide our unique, high-quality, and necessary services to the artists and arts organizations throughout Chicago and Illinois.

Lawyers for the Creative Arts

Jan Feldman, Executive Director
Marci Rolnik Walker, Legal Director
William E. Rattner, Senior Counsel
Sarah Concannon, Administrator

Introduction

Making music is arguably the most rewarding reason to be in a band. Performing live can also be thrilling. But, unless you take care of the business side of your musical passion, you may not be able to pay the bills. To put yourself in the best position to do so, you must take care of all of the legal issues that confront a band—from its formation through breaking up.

This book was written to help you understand and address the most common legal issues that emerge with a band. We have not written this book to be a comprehensive analysis of the legal issues. And given the rapidly shifting dynamics of the music industry, new issues emerge seemingly every day involving various digital technologies and new business models. Huge treatises and textbooks have been published that address all the details and minutiae of the music industry, and they are updated regularly. This book addresses at an introductory level the fundamental issues bands face, including entering into a partnership agreement, song ownership rights, licensing issues, registering copyrights and negotiating recording contracts.

We hope you can use this book as a first resource when wondering what the law may say about a particular issue. And as we mention throughout this book, times will emerge when you should consult with an attorney for advice or to handle a particular situation. But if you keep this book handy, you should be able at least to recognize some of the important issues your band faces, and handle them with knowledge and confidence . . . just how your band performs on stage night after night!

Chapter 1

Do We Need a Partnership Agreement?

You and your buddies recently started a band. You all get along, trust each other, and your focus is on making great music. But, you also realize your band is a business and the legal issues are complex. The first question we usually get as lawyers for musicians who have recently formed a band is, "Do we need a partnership agreement?" The fact that you are asking this question is a good sign. Without treating your band as a business from the get-go, you could wind up in a battle with your bandmates down the road. The choice of whether to operate as a partnership or some other legal entity is a separate question that we touch on briefly below and in more detail in Chapter 10. But, no matter what legal entity your band chooses, **you should attempt to enter into an agreement, often called an "band agreement," setting out the expectations of the group regarding how the band will operate.** Without such an agreement, bitter disputes may arise.

The time to sort out the rules is now, while everyone is getting along. Waiting for an issue to arise before doing so is a recipe for an early breakup. For example, who owns your band name that may have been suggested by the lead singer, but popularized by the group? What if your drummer skips practices and only shows up for gigs? What happens if he skips a gig? What happens when your guitarist leaves the group; can he continue using the name? Can he perform the music he was part of creating? What about the T-shirt design that the bassist came up with—who can use that design if there is a breakup?

The place to address these issues is in the band agreement. If these issues are not addressed in the band agreement, the law will answer them for you. And the law might not provide the answer that you were expecting. For example, unless agreed otherwise, if your drummer misses a gig, he is still entitled to his share of the profits as a part owner of the business. As to the band name, the band owns that name—not any individual member.

> ## *Battle of the Bands:*
> ## When Bandmates Clash
>
> The Beach Boys spent years fighting in court, until they finally settled their lawsuit over the rights of certain band members to use the band's name. The Black Crowes endured a bitter lawsuit over a former manager's claim to an equal portion of the band's profits—based on a pie chart scribbled on a piece of paper during the band's early days of existence. Chris Daughtry, made famous on the hit show *American Idol*, was sued by his former bandmates over songwriting credits. These stories—and many more like them—all occurred because the business details of the bands were not nailed down from the start.

Fundamental issues you want to address in a band agreement include:

- Band member jobs and responsibilities;
- How to split profits from gigs;
- How to split merchandise profits;
- How your band should make future decisions (majority vote or unanimous vote);
- How to determine songwriting credits;
- Who owns the band name; and
- What to do if a band member wants to quit.

An attorney can assist you in drafting an band agreement; however, there is no set way in which these issues must be drafted in an agreement, and you can generally address them how you and your band members agree. We have included a sample band agreement, similar to one which we used with one of our clients, as Appendix A in the back of this book. We do recommend, however, that you consult with an attorney to draft and tailor an agreement to meet your band's specific needs.

As to the legal entity you might want for your band's business, most states provide three relevant options:

(1) A general partnership;

(2) A corporation; or

(3) A limited liability company (LLC).

If your band has been paid for playing a gig, recorded a song, or sold some merchandise, you are likely already recognized as a partnership under the law. A partnership is basically the default legal enterprise that can exist without any formal filing or paperwork. Most states define a partnership as two or more people acting as co-owners of a business for profit. Generally speaking, a partnership exposes its partners to personal liability, while a corporation provides some immunity from personal liability. In Chapter 10, we discuss some of the differences in these legal entities in more detail. But, until such time as personal liability begins to become a concern, you are probably fine continuing to operate as a partnership. Whatever type of legal entity you ultimately choose, however, will require that you have a band agreement.

Chapter 2

Should We Trademark Our Band Name?

It probably was not long after you came together as a group of musicians to create music that the conversation turned to your band's name. You all settled on a name and were proud and excited about it. You should be, as this is your new musical identity. A question we often get from bands like yours is, "Should we trademark our band name?" Again, if your band is asking this question, that is a good sign.

The good news is that a band name can be protected as a trademark. A trademark is a word, phrase, logo, or other characteristic that indicates to consumers that your band is the source of particular goods (albums, T-shirts, posters, etc.) or services (such as live shows). In fact, a band or musician's name can be quite valuable. For example, Elvis Presley Enterprises owns numerous registrations for the "Elvis" trademark and many other trademarks which incorporate the word "Elvis." Licensing these "Elvis" trademarks appears to be big business, as the official Elvis website even features a page devoted solely to providing information about how to license the Elvis name for various goods or services.

So, given the potential monetary value in your band's name and its ability to distinguish you as the source of your music, you are smart to be concerned about protecting your name.

Trademark Rights Arise Through Use of the Mark

Rights in your name as a trademark (sometimes referred to as a "mark") can be created simply by being the first person or business to use it. You may not have to do anything else to obtain rights to your name in the geographic area in which you are using it—just keep on using it.

For example, say that you are the first band to use the name Kicking Picks, and you are doing gigs in Illinois. If no one else has filed for or obtained a federal trademark on the name, filed an intent-to-use federal trademark application, or has an Illinois trademark registration, you will have rights to the name Kicking Picks in Illinois. As you expand into other states, if no state or federal trademark applications have been filed for your name, your rights will grow without having to do anything else but use the name in those areas. If you do well, and use the name across the nation, you could obtain rights across the nation without doing anything but using the name. However, unless you obtain a federal trademark, if you have been using the name only in Illinois, and someone begins using the name in California, like you, they could obtain rights in California.

Benefits of a Federal Trademark Registration

A federal trademark, often called a federal trademark registration (which refers to the fact that the trademark is registered with the United States Patent and Trademark Office), provides the exclusive right to use that trademark throughout the country. Such use is subject only to any prior users, who would be limited to using the trademark in the area in which they had been using it. In the example above, if the band in California were to obtain a federal trademark registration to the name Kicking Picks, that registration would be subject to your right to continue using the name in Illinois. Alternatively, if you obtain a federal trademark registration after they began using the name (and they have not yet started to obtain a federal trademark registration), you would have exclusive rights everywhere in the United States except California.

Clearing Your Trademark

So, it may have dawned on you that the questions you should be asking are: does any band already have a federal trademark in our name, and does anyone else already have rights in the name we selected in certain areas? You can conduct a search to determine if any other bands exist with the same or a similar name. A trademark search can be conducted in several ways. You could perform the search yourself, using the Internet to search the United States Patent and Trademark Office's ("USPTO") trademark database at its website (www.uspto.gov) for possible uses of your name. You can also look for other possible uses of your name through an internet search. These are free ways to conduct a search that can often provide a solid basis to determine whether other parties are using your proposed band name.

An alternative to conducting a search on your own is to hire an attorney to conduct one for you, or to use a trademark search firm (an attorney would most likely use a service like this). A trademark search firm report will show trademark registrations that are the same or similar to your band name, as well as uses of the same or similar name on website domain names and in business listings. Such a report costs several hundred dollars, but it is thorough and can provide a solid basis to determine whether trademark registration of your band name is possible.

These searches, of course, may produce results that show other uses of the name. An issue to consider is whether the uses of the name that come up in your search are for a band, other entertainment goods or services, or goods or services that may not be related to a band or music. This is because trademark rights exist only for the types of goods and services that are specified in the trademark registration, and similar goods or services. For example, say that no other band is using the name Kicking Picks, but the name is being used by a toothpick manufacturer. Because your goods and services as a band are completely different than the goods sold by the toothpick manufacturer, the law presumes that a consumer would most likely not believe that the toothpick manufacturer is the source of your music, and vice versa. Therefore, the existence of this company should not be an impediment to your trademark registration.

As with many aspects of the law, however, an exception to this concept exists. If a mark has become "famous"—think brands such as Coca-Cola, McDonald's, or Microsoft—the owner of this famous mark has the right to stop other uses of the mark that may dilute or tarnish the famous mark. Therefore, to avoid such conflicts, you should not adopt a name that is the same as or confusingly similar to a famous trademark.

Even if you do find another band using the same or a confusingly similar name, unless they have a federal trademark registration, this is not necessarily fatal to your use of the name, or even your obtaining a federal registration to the name. However, you may end up co-existing with a band having a similar name (albeit most likely based in another part of the country).

The Interstate Use Requirement

As alluded to above, to obtain your federal trademark you must use the mark in interstate commerce. This means that the commercial activity associated with the mark is not limited to one state. In today's digital world, using a band's name in interstate commerce is common, as almost every band has a website on which it sells music, or sells its music through a third-party website. Also, any touring or merchandise or album sales in more than one state should be a use in commerce.

However, if you perform in only one state, and do not sell music or in any way use your name outside of that state, you most likely cannot receive a federal trademark for your band name. You could, however, apply for a trademark in the state in which you use the mark, which would provide you protection in that state. Similarly, you can file a federal intent-to-use application, which states that you plan to use the band name in interstate commerce. An intent-to-use application will give you exclusive rights from the date the intent-to-use application is filed provided you begin using the name in interstate commerce within six months, and convert your intent-to-use application to a use-based application (one which states that you are now using the mark in interstate commerce).

The Immoral Mark Issue

Another potential obstacle to federal trademark registration is the prohibition on marks that are "immoral, deceptive, or scandalous," or that disparage or bring into disrepute a person or institution. No defined test exists as to what may constitute immoral, deceptive, or scandalous material. However, if your band's name contains profanity, explicit drug references, or explicit sexual references, it is possible that you will be denied a federal trademark registration.

Whether or not you could be denied a federal trademark registration if your band name clearly insults a person or institution is the subject of debate. The Trademark Office recently cancelled the Washington Redskins' trademark registration on the basis that it contained matter that may disparage a substantial composite of Native Americans, and a federal court upheld that decision. The Redskins have appealed the federal court decision. In their appeal, the Redskins are arguing that the prohibition on disparaging trademarks violates a person's right to free speech because it allows the government to ban content based solely on the possibility that some might find the content offensive. In the meantime, another federal court has recently ruled that the prohibition on disparaging trademarks is unconstitutional for the same reasons argued by the Redskins. The court reviewing the Redskins' case is not bound by the other court's decision, but the Supreme Court recently decided to review the other court's decision. The Supreme Court's decision, on the other hand, will control the outcome of the Redskin's case. For now, the prohibition on disparaging trademarks is still good law in certain parts of the country. So, for safe measure, and to avoid alienating any fans, it is probably good practice to avoid band names that insult a person or institution.

When Trademarks Met Hard Rock: The Tale of Ozzy Osbourne and the "Black Sabbath" Name

Ozzy Osbourne may be best-known for his wild and outrageous rock-'n'-roll antics and lifestyle. He can also serve as an example of a musician who did not recognize until far too late the value in owning a trademark to his band name, in his case the pioneering hard rock band Black Sabbath.

Black Sabbath formed in 1969, and broke up in the 1980s. According to Black Sabbath guitarist Tony Iommi, when Ozzy left the group in 1980, he signed an agreement in which he gave up his rights to the "Black Sabbath" name. In 1999, Iommi filed an application with the USPTO to register "Black Sabbath" as a trademark. In 2000, when the USPTO approved the application for the "Black Sabbath" trademark, Iommi obtained the exclusive right to use the band name in the United States for uses such as performing concerts and selling merchandise and CDs.

In 2008 Iommi sued concert promoter Live Nation and Signature Network—the company that had licensed the "Black Sabbath" mark for merchandise—for trademark infringement related to their uses of the "Black Sabbath" mark. After Iommi had taken action in federal court, Ozzy filed his own federal lawsuit, and asked the court to rule that he was a co-owner of the "Black Sabbath" mark. After all, Ozzy was the lead singer and face of the band, and Ozzy and Iommi had been splitting royalties for merchandise sales since their 1997 reunion tour. Ozzy and his wife, Sharon Osbourne, also ran the blacksabbath.com website.

Forty years after Ozzy and Iommi had joined forces to pioneer the hard rock landscape with Black Sabbath, they were battling before a judge over who owned this valuable name. And they had plenty at stake, given that Black Sabbath had sold millions of albums and earned millions more from touring and merchandise sales. A good band agreement, as discussed in Chapter 1, may have prevented this battle.

Bad blood can sometimes sour relationships in a band. But Ozzy and Iommi worked out their differences and reached an amicable settlement. Black Sabbath returned to touring, headlining concerts such as the 2012 Lollapalooza in Chicago, and recorded a new album. Fortunately, the fight over the "Black Sabbath" name apparently did not leave lasting scars.

Trademarking Last Names

While trademark law states that a last name usually cannot be registered as a mark, it is possible for an artist to register his or her name as a trademark if it is recognized by consumers when they see or hear it as the source of particular goods or services. For example, the band Van Halen owns several federal registrations for the "Van Halen" mark, even though this is the last name of two of the band's original members. It obtained these registrations because its name had become well-known on account of the band's success, and the fact that it had used its name continuously for at least five years. This is how other groups such as the Dave Matthews Band or artists such as Bob Dylan obtained trademarks for their names—their success allowed them to prove that their names had become well-known.

The Process of Obtaining a Trademark

If you choose to pursue a federal trademark registration for your name, this can be done without an attorney, and resources exist at the USPTO's website at uspto.gov to help with the registration process. Alternatively, a trademark attorney can assist in this process and let you focus on your music. In 2016, obtaining a federal trademark, if you do it by yourself, can cost as little as $225 (for one class of goods/services). However, you will likely want to file your registration for at least two classes: Class 41, Education and Entertainment Services, and Class 9, Scientific Apparatus (for CDs and digital downloads).

Protecting Your Trademark

Once you have registered your mark, you must continue to use your trademark in order to maintain your rights. If you stop using the band name—say the band breaks up or changes names—your rights to the mark will expire. You must also comply with the USPTO's renewal obligations. To do so, you must file an affidavit with the USPTO in the year before the six-year anniversary of your mark's registration and in the year before the 10-year anniversary of your mark's registration. In this affidavit, you must state that you are still using the mark in commerce for the goods and services that are set forth in your mark's registration, or that you have an excusable reason why you are temporarily not using the mark.

You should also use your trademark in a consistent manner. For example, if you have registered a logo as a trademark, you should use the same logo or very similar derivations of the logo. You should also use your name in the same way. You should avoid adding, deleting, or changing words in your name. Changing your name will only reduce the ability of the name to identify your band as the source of your music. However, if you do change your band's name, you can apply to register this new name as a trademark, and let the old mark expire.

Finally, you should police uses of your mark or similar versions of your mark. If you allow other bands or entertainers to use the same or confusingly similar versions of your name, you run the risk of your trademark becoming generic or weak. If you discover someone else using a name that is likely to be confused with your name, you should at least write them a letter demanding that they stop using the name. And, you should be prepared to file a lawsuit against them if they do not comply. Note that these actions would most likely require you to hire an attorney.

While obligations certainly exist if you own a trademark to your band name, the benefits you receive if you own the mark usually outweigh the obligations.

Numerous musicians and bands own trademarks for their names. Beyoncé, Madonna, Kanye West, Bon Jovi, The Rolling Stones, Radiohead, the Black Eyed Peas, and Bruce Springsteen are just a few of the artists and bands who own such marks. Bands also own trademarks to graphics or logos that have become synonymous with the group, such as the Grateful Dead's "steal your face" skull with a lightning bolt running through it. Even the name of one of this country's great cities, Boston, is a registered trademark for the classic rock group (and one that has been subject to litigation, as the band's founder sued one of the group's former guitarists for continuing to use the band's name to promote his career long after he left the group).

For sure, these are examples of music superstars and legends securing trademarks. These artists understand that their names are valuable intellectual property, and that a trademark provides them the exclusive right to use their names. However, trademarks are not reserved just for stars. Millions of dollars need not be at stake for a name to receive trademark protection. **Any band can and should attempt to register its name as a trademark.** Your name can be one of your most valuable assets, the "brand" under which you create, distribute, and perform music.

Chapter 3

Who Owns Our Music?

Those long nights and weekends spent in your band's small and loud rehearsal space have paid off. Random guitar riffs and horn lines have evolved into melodic and cohesive songs with hard-driving and danceable rhythms. Words brainstormed and jotted into a tattered notebook and typed into your iPhone now tell the stories for a new album. Your band not only has developed a personal and unique sound, but it now has its own song catalog. But who "owns" these songs?

One or two compositions may have been written almost entirely by a single band member; others may have involved substantial contributions by a couple members and minor, but important, input from one or two others; others were pure collaborative works where one person came up with the hook, and the entire band built a composition around it. Everyone performed the compositions on the band's album.

The starting point in discussing ownership of your band's music is a fundamental concept in copyright law that can often lead to confusion—**there are two separate and distinct copyrights in a song. First, there is a copyright for the "composition" itself. These are the musical notes, lyrics, and the arrangement. Another entirely distinct copyright exists in the "sound recording." This is the recording of a composition** that is placed on an album, sold as an MP3, or broadcast over the radio. The sound recording is the actual recorded performance of the composition. We will address rights to each specific work in this section.

Ownership in Your Compositions

Since compositions are usually created before sound recordings, let's begin by sorting out who owns the compositions. A band's most valuable assets can be its compositions. Think of the millions in royalties that legendary songwriters like George Gershwin and Harold Arlen earned for classics such as "Summertime" and "Over The Rainbow," respectively. Or the millions earned by songwriting teams like Lennon & McCartney, Jimmy Jam and Terry Lewis, and whoever wrote all of those pop songs for Britney Spears. Composition ownership can be a big business, and even a small ownership percentage can mean real money if the composition makes it big. Absent a band agreement that controls ownership, copyright law governs the question of who owns the compositions. But, copyright law does not always lead to a simple answer.

When two or more people create a composition with "the intention that their contributions be merged into inseparable or interdependent parts of a unitary whole," the work is a joint work. **Under the Copyright Act, absent an agreement to the contrary, each joint author has equal ownership in the work, each has the right to individually exploit the work (such as license it), and each has a duty to account to the other owners for profits they individually obtain from exploiting the work.**

Some courts insist that even if you intend to create joint ownership of the works, each person has to contribute some copyrightable expression to the composition. But, the Supreme Court has set the bar low as to what constitutes copyrightable subject matter—it basically has to have more creativity and originality than listings in a White Pages phone book. Further, other courts find collaborators joint authors even if one of the collaborators did not create independently copyrightable expression. Sorting out who contributed what after the fact is often difficult, and **the safest course is to assume that absent an agreement to the contrary all contributors will have an equal claim**

of ownership to the composition. If a different result is desired, a written agreement is necessary.

Sometimes, bands agree that the compositions will be owned by the contributing members based upon the amount contributed to the composition. For example, perhaps the lead singer/guitarist wrote the lyrics, came up with the melodies, and crafted the song structure. Maybe the drummer and bassist simply crafted their parts around the guitarist's composition, and the rhythm guitarist just played the part that was given to him. Unless your band wants each contributing author to be considered an equal owner of the composition, you should agree that the composition will be owned based upon contribution and, for every composition, determine the percentage of the composition owned by each band member.

This agreement can be reflected in a simple letter (a sample is attached as Appendix B at the back of this book) assigning ownership for each composition in proportion to each band member's contribution. Such a letter should be done for each of your band's compositions (or one letter for several compositions). Make sure that the letter is dated, and that each member of the band signs the letter, regardless of what percentage, if any, he or she owns of the composition.

On the other hand, absent an agreement to the contrary, only the members who actually contributed to the composition own the rights to the composition. Sometimes, bands choose to require all authors to assign their compositions to the band. Then, each band member would have an ownership interest in the compositions through his or her ownership of the band, or the band could agree that (while it owns the compositions) all revenue derived from the compositions will be distributed to the co-authors. This approach may help streamline the copyright registration process discussed in Chapter 4 below. However your band decides to handle ownership of the compositions, it should be set out in the band agreement.

A word of caution to those bands that choose to give composition credit (albeit in small percentages) to certain individuals. After 35 years, any joint author could potentially terminate that agreement and recapture its full share of ownership rights. It is important to understand this aspect of copyright law before choosing to collaborate with someone on your composition.

Publishing Companies

Musicians often license their compositions to publishing companies. Publishing companies attempt to generate revenue by licensing your compositions. Bands may own their own publishing companies and publish their compositions with this company. Or, a band may license its compositions to a larger publishing company, which can help it get royalties for compositions and get compositions placed in media such as commercials and movies. For example, major multinational publishing companies such as Sony/ATV Music Publishing and Warner/Chappell Music own and control the publishing rights to millions of musical compositions, including classic compositions from legendary songwriters as well as those from some of today's newest stars.

Smaller publishing companies have also emerged as the music industry moves away from a centralized major label model to a more egalitarian, indie-driven business. And, as discussed in Chapter 5, compositions can mean big business, as they can provide steady sources of income. For example, every time an artist records a cover version of another artist's composition, the owner of the composition collects a royalty.

Ownership in Your Sound Recordings

Regarding your sound recordings, ownership is a little more clear-cut. Unless your band's band agreement provides otherwise, those who perform the song are joint authors of the sound recording. Additionally, absent an agreement to the contrary, producers and sound engineers may be considered co-authors of the sound recording. However, by agreement, record labels often obtain ownership of the copyright in the sound recordings, or they may require the artists to license the sound recordings exclusively to the record label. In return, the record label should be required to market and promote these albums and pay its artists royalties for the albums that it sells.

By owning or being the exclusive licensee of the sound recordings, record labels have the financial incentive to promote their artists when they release their albums. As discussed in Chapter 5, a recording can be a valuable asset and a steady source of income from album and song sales, licenses to sample the recording, or licenses to use the recording in television shows, commercials, movies, or other media.

If your band chooses to retain ownership of its sound recordings rather than license them to a record label, you could require each author to transfer his or her rights in the sounds recordings to the band, and have the band own the copyrights to the recordings. The approach you use will impact how you complete the copyright registrations, as discussed in Chapter 4, so it is important to make this decision early.

Even though discussing who owns your band's music may not be easy, it is an important part of formalizing the working relationship between your bandmates, and those that help to capture your band's performances. It may not be as enjoyable as making music, but it is an important part of having a good working relationship and preventing future fights.

Transferring Ownership

There are two primary ways in which a band that creates compositions or sound recordings transfers the rights to this music to another party. The manner selected may have significant consequences.

The first way to transfer ownership in a copyright would be through a copyright assignment agreement, which is a written document that, for example, transfers the rights to sound recordings to a record label. Such an agreement could also be used for individual members of your band to transfer ownership of the compositions they write, and their interest in the sound recordings, to the band itself.

The other method occurs under the work-made-for-hire doctrine. Under the work-made-for-hire doctrine, if someone is employed to create a work, their work is owned by the employer; in essence, the work is transferred to the employer when it is created. Sometimes, bands seek to transfer compositions and sound recordings to the band by employing each of the members to create compositions and record music. Similarly, many recording companies purport in their record deals to employ the band to create sound recordings. Importantly, however, in deciding whether such work-made-for-hire agreements are enforceable, courts will evaluate whether the authors actually were employees. As such, many agreements are written as work-made-for hire and copyright assignment agreements (in case a court determines the work was not actually crated by an employee).

There are two major consequences which flow from the manner in which a company obtains ownership of a copyright. First, how these rights are transferred to a third party affects the length during which these works can be protected by copyright. Copyright protection begins at the moment a work is created and typically endures for the term of the author's life plus an additional 70 years after the author's death. ("Author" means the person who created the work.) Or, if two or more people jointly created the work, the copyright protection term lasts for 70 years after the last surviving author's death. If a band or record label obtains ownership by assignment, the copyright endures for this entire period. Consider a twenty-year-old band member that lives to be 80-the life of the copyright would be 150 years! But, if a band or record label obtains ownership by virtue of the work-made-for-hire doctrine, the term of the copyright is 95 years from the date of publication (the release of an album, for example) or 120 years from creation, whichever expires first.

Second, as discussed elsewhere in this book, between 35 to 40 years after the grant, copyright assignments can be terminated. If the band or record label obtains ownership under the work-made-for-hire doctrine, however, the grant of ownership cannot be terminated. Given this termination right, it is good practice to document the authors of a band's compositions and the performers of the sound recording, even if the compositions and sound recordings are assigned to the band.

In short, copyrights acquired through assignment may last substantially longer than copyrights aquired under the work-made-for-hire doctrine. But, copyrights acquired by assignment can revert back to the original authors 35 years after they are assigned. If termination is not a serious concern, assignments are the better practice.

Appendices C and D are sample agreements that have been used to transfer compositions and sound recordings from the band member's to the band. Appendix C is a copyright assignment agreement entered into between a band and its members. Appendix D is a work-made-for-hire agreement for a band and its members. Either agreement can be modified such that it only covers sound recordings, leaving ownership of the compositions to the authors as set out in the copyright split sheet.

Chapter 4

Should We Register Our Copyrights, and How?

The vast majority of bands do not have a recording contract. After cutting its first album, which the group paid for on its own, a band wants to know whether it needs to obtain a copyright registration from the Copyright Office, and how it can do so. The good news is that a band does not have to actually register the work to receive copyright protection. Without even knowing it, if you have written down the notes to an original composition or recorded an original track, you already own copyrights in your works. Copyright registration is not a condition of copyright protection. You can have a copyright without even registering it.

Since January 1, 1978, copyright law in the United States has automatically protected a work when it was created. As soon as a work is "fixed" in a copy or phonorecord (a "phonorecord" is the physical object in which works of authorship are embodied; it includes CDs, vinyl, and even MP3s and other digital formats), copyright protection exists for the creator of the work. Neither registration nor publication is a requirement for copyright protection.

Even though registration is unnecessary for a work, many advantages exist to registering copyrights with the U.S. Copyright Office. And it is cheap and relatively easy, so registering your copyrights is a good idea. Some of the advantages of registering your works with the Copyright Office are:

- Registration establishes a public record of the copyright claim;
- If made within five years of publication, registration will establish evidence in court of the validity of the copyright and of the facts stated in the registration certificate (i.e. who wrote the work, and who owns it);
- In order to file a lawsuit for copyright infringement, you must first register your copyright, or in some jurisdictions have a pending registration;

- If registration is made either within three months of publication or prior to an infringement of the work, the copyright owner may receive statutory damages and attorney's fees in a lawsuit. Otherwise, only the actual amount of damages and losses in profit caused by the infringement will be available to the copyright owner. Statutory damages and attorney's fees can be very significant remedies in a copyright infringement lawsuit; and

- Registration of your compositions is required in order to receive compulsory license royalties.

Formalities of Copyright Registration

To register copyrights for your musical compositions and sound recordings, there are three essential elements to completing your application for registration with the U.S. Copyright Office:

(1) A completed application form;

(2) A nonrefundable filing fee, currently $35 for a Single Application or $55 for a Standard Application, both filed online, and $85 if filed by mail; the fees are subject to change. For up-to-date information on fees, check the Copyright Office website at copyright.gov, or call (202) 707-3000 or (877) 476-0778; and

(3) A nonreturnable deposit of your work—that is, you must "deposit" a copy or copies of the work being registered with the Copyright Office.

Registration can usually be done without the assistance of an attorney. Additionally, one application can often be used to obtain protection for several works, which can save a lot of money. The trick is figuring out which and how many works can be protected in one application. In this chapter, we walk you through common copyright scenarios we often see bands encounter.

Single vs. Standard Application

The preferred (and easier) way to register the copyright in your works is online through the Copyright Office's electronic filing system, eCO. eCO offers two types of applications that apply to compositions and sound recordings: the Single Application and the Standard Application. Before you can register your work or works, you first need to determine what type of application you will need to file. Generally, the number of works being registered determines whether you will need to file a Single Application or a Standard Application. If you use the wrong application, your application may take more time to process and you may have to pay additional fees. The Single Application form is used if you are registering one work by a single author who is also the owner. In any other situation, including when you are registering multiple works, you will need to file a Standard Application.

<u>Determining How Many Applications to File: The Three Questions to Ask Yourself Before Registering Your Works</u>

Who is the claimant of the works being registered?

The first thing you will need to determine is the claimant of the copyright in the works. The claimant is the person or entity claiming ownership of the copyright in the works. The author is the original claimant of a work. If there are two or more authors, then the two or more of them are the claimants. Of course, the author(s) can transfer their rights in the work, which is the only way that someone other than the author(s) can become the claimant. As such, the claimant can also be a person or entity to whom the author(s) have legally transferred the copyright in the work. To be named as a claimant, a non-author must own all rights and authorship in the work. In other words, every author must assign her entire right in the work to the claimant. Determining the claimant of the work is important because *multiple works can only be registered on one application if they have the same claimant*, regardless of whether the works have been published or share an author. This is why it can be helpful to assign the ownership in your compositions and sound recordings to the band. By doing so, the band becomes the claimant of both the compositions and the sound recordings, which means that one Standard Application can be used to register both the compositions and the sound recordings, provided the other requirements based on publication status or authorship are met. Often times, only the sound recordings are assigned to the band. In that situation, the sound recordings can be registered together, but the compositions must be protected separately. Therefore, the first question to ask is who is the claimant of the works, and the works should be organized by claimant.

Have the works being registered been published?

After grouping the works by claimant, the next thing to determine is whether the works being registered have been published. The Copyright Act defines "publication" as "the distribution of copies or phonorecords of a work to the public by sale or other transfer of ownership, or by rental, lease, or lending." A "phonorecord" is the physical material in which your music is fixed, such as a CD or vinyl record. Under this definition of "publication," your work is published as soon as you sell or give away CDs, records, or digital copies like MP3s. "Publication" also includes offering to distribute copies or phonorecords of a work to a group of people for further distribution or public performance. This would include asking iTunes or Spotify to upload your music for public access. It is worth noting that "publication" does not include the mere public performance of a work. So, performing all of the songs off your new album at a concert would not be publication, but selling or giving the CD away at that concert would. It is important to note that, technically, once a work is published, the publisher is supposed to provide two copies of the work to the Copyright Office. Failure to do so after receiving a demand from the Copyright Office could lead to fines.

If the works being registered have been published, then the next question is whether the works were published together. Works are published together if they are first published at the same time in a single unit of publication. Selling or giving away a CD of new, original tracks would mean that all of the tracks on that CD were published together, provided that no tracks on the CD had been previously published, because the CD constitutes a single unit of publication.

If the works have the same claimant, and they were published together, the works can be protected with one application.

If not published, who are the authors of each of the works being registered?

For unpublished works, to determine the number of applications, you will need to determine the author or authors for each of the works being registered. This information is actually necessary for filling out all applications. Typically, the author is the creator of the work, *e.g.,*the songwriter(s) of the composition or musician(s) playing on the sound recording. The only exception to this rule is when the work is created as a work-made-for-hire, in which case the employer is considered the author. Authorship is critical because unless there is an agreement stating otherwise, the author is also the owner of the copyright in the work, or the claimant.

Multiple unpublished works can only be registered on the same application if the works being registered have at least one author in common and have the same claimant. In other words, in addition to needing to have the same claimant, at least one author must have contributed to each work.

Answering these three questions will determine how many applications you will need to file in order to register all of your works. While it seems overwhelming, we can actually establish a few simple rules from the information above:

1. A Single Application can only be used if you are registering one work by a single author who is also the claimant;

2. Multiple works can be registered using one Standard Application if those works have the same claimant, and they were either:

   (a) published together; or

   (b) are unpublished works having at least one author in common;

3. If all of the compositions and sound recordings have the same claim-
    ant, they can be registered using one Standard Application as long as
    they either (i) were published together (if they are published), or (ii)
    if not published, have at least one author in common.

The following examples from the Copyright Office's website help dem-
onstrate how to determine the number of applications needed when registering
multiple works:

Examples of <u>published</u> collections:

Again, to register multiple published works on a single registration, the
claimant must be the same and the works must have been first published
together. Consider these examples:

Example 1: CD entitled TORTURED contains 9 songs, all published for
the first time together. The compositions are owned by their respective authors,
but the sound recordings are owned by the band.

Songs 1-8: by Al

Song 9: by Sue

For the copyright in the composition, use separate applications. Each author
owns the copyright only in his or her own song(s). Songs 1-8 can be registered
with one Standard Application naming Al as the author and claimant; Song
9 must be registered separately with a separate Single Application naming
Sue as the author and claimant. For the copyright in the sound recordings, all
songs can be registered with one Standard Application naming Al and Sue as
the authors and their band as the claimant.

Example 2: CD entitled GAME PLAY contains 10 songs. All authors
signed agreements transferring the copyrights in their compositions to Merry
Songs Company, but the sound recordings are owned by the band.

Song 1-4: by Al & Bill

Song 5 & 6: by Mike

Song 7-10: by Linda (song 9 appeared in a previously published CD)

For the copyright in the compositions, use one Standard Application for songs 1-8 and 10 naming Al, Bill, Mike, and Linda as the authors and Merry Songs Company as the claimant. The claimant is the same for all songs because the authors have signed agreements transferring the copyrights in their compositions. For the copyright in the sound recordings, use one Standard Application for songs 1-8 and 10 naming Al, Bill, Mike, and Linda as the authors and their band as the claimant. The claimant is the same for all songs because the sound recordings are owned by the band. (Song 9 should be excluded because it was previously published. It may be registered separately based on the facts of first publication).

Examples of <u>unpublished</u> collections:

For unpublished works to be registered together, the claimant must be the same and the works have to have a common author. Consider these examples:

Example 1: Collection entitled MORE BLUES AND HUES, containing 3 songs. The compositions are owned by their respective authors, but the sound recordings are owned by the band.

Song 1: by Al
Song 2: by Al
Song 3: by Sue

For the copyright in the compositions, use separate applications for Al and Sue. Each author owns the copyright in his or her own song. Al should register his compositions with one Standard Application naming himself as the author and claimant; Sue may register her composition separately with a Single Application naming herself as the author and claimant. For the copyright in the sound recordings, use one application. While no one author contributed to every composition, presumably Al and Sue recorded all three songs together. As such, both Al and Sue would be authors on all three sound recordings. And, the sound recordings all have the same claimant because the rights in the sounds recordings were transferred to the band. Songs 1-3 can be registered on one Standard Application naming Al and Sue as the authors and the band as the claimant.

Example 2: Collection entitled HUNKER DOWN, containing 4 songs. The compositions are owned by their respective authors, but the sound recordings are owned by the band.

Song 1: by Al & Bill
Song 2: by Al & Bill
Song 3: by Al
Song 4: by Al

For the copyright in the compositions, use separate applications. Even though one author did write or cowrite every song, the claimant of all the compositions is not the same. Al and Bill can register compositions 1 and 2 with one Standard Application naming themselves as authors and claimants; Al can register compositions 3 and 4 with a separate Standard Application naming himself as the author and claimant. For the copyright in the sound recordings, use one Standard Application naming Al and Bill as the authors and the band as the claimaint. Al contributed to all 4 songs and the sound recordings have the same claimant because the rights were transferred to the band.

Example 3: CD entitled LIFE PATTERNS contains 3 songs. All authors signed agreements transferring the copyrights in their compositions to Merry Songs Company, but the sound recordings are owned by the band.

Song 1: by Al & Bill
Song 2: by Al
Song 3: by Al & Sue

For the copyright in the compositions, use one Standard Application naming Al, Bill, and Sue as the authors and Merry Songs Company as the claimant. One of the authors contributed to every song, and the claimaint is the same for all of the compositions because the authors transferred their rights to Merry Songs Company. For the copyright in the sound recordings, use one Standard Application naming Al, Bill, and Sue as the authors and the band as the claimaint. One of the authors contributed to every song, and the claimaint is the same for all of the sound recordings because the authors transferred their rights to the band.

One more example ...

Assume a band released one album and is about to release another. All songs on both albums are new and original. The authors individually own the compositions in proportion to their contribution, and the band owns the sound recordings. The first album had 10 songs: Artist A was an author on songs 1-6 and 10; Artist B was an author on songs 5-8 and 10; Artist C wrote song 9; and Artist D was an author on song 10. The second album had 10 songs: Artist A was an author on songs 1-6 and 10; Artist B was an author on songs 5-8 and 10; Artist C wrote song 9; and Artist D was an author on song 10. In order to obtain copyright protection for each composition and recording, how many applications would need to be filed?

<u>Album 1</u>

Song 1: by A	Song 6: by A & B
Song 2: by A	Song 7: by B
Song 3: by A	Song 8: by B
Song 4: by A	Song 9: by C
Song 5: by A & B	Song 10: by A, B, & D

The first album is published because the band has released the album. Further, the songs were all first published together because all of the songs are new and original. As seen in our rules above, this means that the songs on the first album can be registered together provided they have the same claimant. The claimants for the compositions will be the authors because there has not been any transfer of rights in the compositions. Thus, the compositions can only be registered together if they have the same authors. The claimant for the sound recordings, on the other hand, will be the band. This means that the sound recordings can be registered together.

For the copyright in the compositions, use five separate applications: Songs 1-4 can be registered on one Standard Application naming Artist A as the author and claimant; Songs 5-6 can be registered on one Standard Application naming Artists A and B as the authors and claimants; Songs 7-8 can be registered on one Standard Application naming Artist B as the author and claimant; Song 9 can be registered on a Single Application naming Artist C as the author and claimant; Song 10 can be registered on a Standard Application naming Artists A, B, and D as the authors and claimants.

For the copyright in the sound recording, use one Standard Application naming Artist A, B, C, and D as the authors and the band as the claimant.

<u>Album 2</u>

Song 1: by A	Song 6: by A & B
Song 2: by A	Song 7: by B
Song 3: by A	Song 8: by B
Song 4: by A	Song 9: by C
Song 5: by A & B	Song 10: by A, B, & D

The second album is not published because the band has not released the album yet. As seen in our rules above, this means that the songs on the second album can be registered together provided they have the same claimaint and at least one author in common. The claimants for the compositions will be the authors because there has not been any transfer of rights in the compositions. Thus, the compositions can only be registered together if they have the same authors, and one of those author contributed to each work. The claimant for the sound recordings, on the other hand, will be the band. This means that the sound recordings can only be registered together if at least one author contributed to each sound recording on that particular registration.

For the copyright in the compositions, use five separate applications: Songs 1-4 can be registered on one Standard Application naming Artist A as the author and claimant; Songs 5-6 can be registered on one Standard Application naming Artists A and B as the authors and claimants; Songs 7-8 can be registered on one Standard Application naming Artist B as the author and claimant; Song 9 can be registered on a Single Application naming Artist C as the author and claimant; Song 10 can be registered on a Standard Application naming Artists A, B, and D as the authors and claimants.

For the copyright in the sound recordings, if at least one author performed on every song, use one application naming Artists A, B, C, and D as the authors and the band as the claimant.

Thus, to answer our question, it would take a total of twelve applications to obtain copyright protection for all of the compositions and sound recordings across these two albums. All of the information in each application must be correct, or else you will face delays with the Copyright Office. And while a lot of the information is the same, there will be subtle differences in the places where the information is provided in each application. This is why it is so important to figure exactly how many registrations you will need to file and which works will be registered in each application before you begin your registration.

As seen in the examples, determining how many applications you will need to file is easy if you use the three rules outlined above. But, sometimes the real world can be a bit more complex than the relatively simple examples provided. For more complex problems with registration, the flow chart on the next page will help determine how many applications you will need to file if you are registering multiple works.

Electronic Federal Registration for Compositions and Sound Recordings

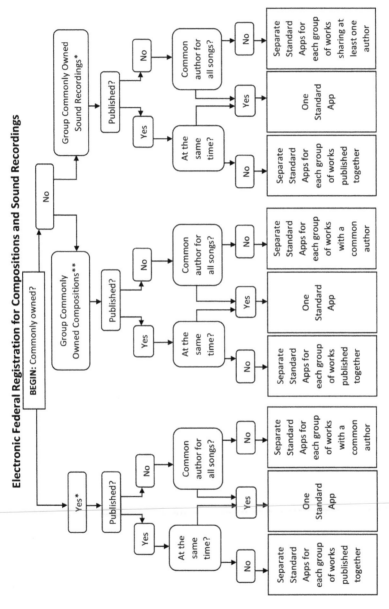

* Indicate the "Type of Work" is a "Sound Recording" (even if you are registering both compositions and sound recordings)

** Indicate the "Type of Work" is a "Work of the Performing Arts"

Registering Your Works Online

Now that we've discussed how to determine the number of applications you will need to file, let's turn to the process of using eCO to register your works online. This tutorial will use the following facts:

Say, for example, your band is named the Chicago Commuters. You have recorded and released the album Crosstown Boogie with eight new, original tracks: "Positively Clark Street," "Halsted Street Shuffle," "Logan Boulevard of Broken Dreams," "North Avenue Freeze-Out," "On Green Kedzie Street," "Going Down Irving Park Road Feeling Bad," "Rock On To Fullerton Avenue," and "No Sleep Till Pilsen." The compositions were not written together, but rather each composition was written separately by some combination of group members Joe Guitarist, Barbara Singer, and Larry Drummer. However, all rights to the compositions and sound recordings have been transferred to the band's corporate identity, the Chicago Commuters LLC.

A breakdown of the tracks might look something like this:

Album:	Crosstown Boogie				
Artist:	The Chicago Commuters				
Track No.	Title of Work	Composition Author(s)	Sound Recording Authors	Published	Claimant
1	"Positively Clark Street"	Joe Guitarist	All	Yes	Chicago Commuters LLC
2	"Halsted Street Shuffle"	Joe Guitarist Barbara Singer	All	Yes	Chicago Commuters LLC
3	"Logan Boulevard of Broken Dreams"	Barbara Singer	All	Yes	Chicago Commuters LLC
4	"North Avenue Freeze-Out"	Larry Drummer	All	Yes	Chicago Commuters LLC
5	"On Green Kedzie Street"	Joe Guitarist Larry Drummer	All	Yes	Chicago Commuters LLC
6	"Going Down Irving Park Road Feeling Bad"	Barbara Singer Larry Drummer	All	Yes	Chicago Commuters LLC
7	"Rock on to Fullerton Avenue"	Joe Guitarist Barbara Singer Larry Drummer	All	Yes	Chicago Commuters LLC
8	"No Sleep Till Pilsen"	Joe Guitarist	All	Yes	Chicago Commuters LLC

We can see from the breakdown that we need to register multiple published works (the works are published because the Chicago Commuters recorded *and released* the album). Turning to our rule for multiple published works, we know that all of the works can be registered on the same application if those works were published together and have the same claimant. The works were published together because they were all released for the first time on the album *Crosstown Boogie*. The works also have the same claimant because the rights in the compositions and the sound recordings have been transferred to the Chicago Commuters LLC. This also means that both the compositions and sound recordings can be registered in one Standard Application. Now, lets walk through the steps to register these works using eCO.

Create an Account

Before you can register any works, you will need to go to the "copyright.gov" website and create an account with eCO. There is nothing special about creating an account, and you only need to provide some basic information and a username and password. If you already have an account, you will need to login to eCO from the copyright.gov website.

Begin Registering Your Work

To begin registering your works, you will need to click on the "Register a New Claim" link found in the column on the left side of the page.

After clicking "Register a New Claim," you will be prompted to answer three questions. These questions help you determine if you should be filing a Single Application or a Standard Application. As mentioned above, the Single Application can only be used to register one work with a single author who is also the claimant. Answering "No" to any of these three questions means that you cannot use the Single Application. In our case, we are registering multiple works with multiple authors, so the answer to all three questions is "No." Once you have answered all three questions, click the "Start Registration" button.

Check Registration Case Status

Open Cases
Working Cases
All Cases
My Company's Cases
Status Definitions
Search My Cases
My Applications
My Company's Applications

Copyright Registration

Register a New Claim
Preregister a Claim
Register a Group Claim
Use a Template
Organization / DA

Additional Copyright Services

Access Copyright Office Information
- Ask a Question?
- Read Circulars
- Search Online Records

Register a claim in 3 steps in the following order: (1) Complete an application, (2) Make payment, (3) Send us a copy of your work.

To begin, please answer the following questions about the work(s) you are registering, then click the "Start Registration" button. Your answers to these questions will determine the appropriate application for registering your work.

Yes   No

☑   Are you registering one work (one song, one poem, one illustration, etc.)? Check " NO " to this question if the work is one of the following: a collection of works (such as: book of poetry, CD of songs and photographs), a collective work, website or database because these works do not qualify for the single form.

☑   Are you the only author and owner of the work (or the agent of the individual author who is also the only owner)?

☑   Does the work you are sending contain material created only by this author? Check "NO" to this question if the copy includes content or contributions by anyone else, even if the claim is limited to only the contribution by this author or the material has been licensed, permissioned or transferred to the claimant.

You should now see the first page for the eCO electronic form:

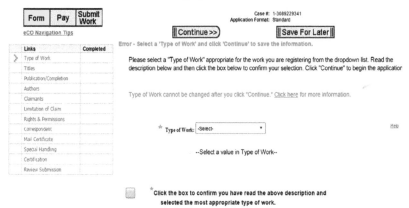

eCO will now take you through a series of pages that look very similar to the first page. Each of these pages will contain a separate fillable form related to different pieces of information necessary to complete your application. Once you have filled in all the required fields (indicated with a red asterisk), you will have completed the form. The separate pages, and your progress through them, are displayed in a column on the left side of the page:

Links	Completed
Type of Work	
Titles	
Publication/Completion	
Authors	
Claimants	
Limitation of Claim	
Rights & Permissions	
Correspondent	
Mail Certificate	
Special Handling	
Certification	
Review Submission	

Type of Work

The first thing you need to do is indicate the type of work you are registering. There are several options found in a drop down menu in the middle of the page. If you click on each individual option a brief description will appear. For all purposes of registering musical compositions and sound recording, there are only two relevant options. First, a musical composition should be registered as a "Work of the Performing Arts." Second, a sound recording should be registered as a "Sound Recording." **When you are registering both musical compositions and sound recordings in one application, as we are in our example, you should select "Sound Recording."**

After you have completed all required fields, click the "Continue" button to be taken to the next page.

Titles

The next thing you will need to do is to give the titles of the works being registered. For each title you are adding, first click the "New" button. You will then be taken to a page for entering the title of the work. When you are registering multiple works, you have to register them as a Collection of Works. Unfortunately, there is no option to directly register a Collection of Works. Rather, you need to register the collection (*i.e.*, the album) as the work being registered and list the names of the individual songs on that CD as the contents of the collection. To do this, after clicking the "New" button, the first thing you should do is enter the name of your album as the "Title of work being registered:"

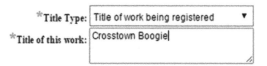

You will then need to add each individual song on the album. You do this by clicking the "New" button and entering the name of the song as a "Contents Title:"

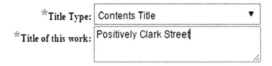

You will need to do this for every song on the album:

Title of Work ⇕	Volume ⇕	Number ⇕	Issue Date ⇕	Type ⇕
Crosstown Boogie				Title of work being registered
Positively Clark Street				Contents Title
Halsted Street Shuffle				Contents Title
Logan Boulevard of Broken Dreams				Contents Title
North Avenue Freeze-Out				Contents Title
On Green Kedzie Street				Contents Title
Going Down Irving Park Road Feeling Bad				Contents Title
Rock on to Fullerton Avenue				Contents Title
No Sleep Till Pilsen				Contents Title

After you have completed all required fields, click the "Continue" button to be taken to the next page.

Publication/Completion

To complete this section, first indicate whether the works being registered have been published. In our case, the works have been published, so we are required to enter the date of completion of the works and the date of publication. For the date of publication, enter the date your works were first published in accordance with the definition of publication discussed above.

After you have completed all required fields, click the "Continue" button to be taken to the next page.

Authors

For each author you are adding, first click the "New" button just as you did for the titles of the works. You will then be taken to a separate page, and you must add the required author information for each author one-by-one. It is worth noting that you will need to know the citizenship or domicile of each author, as it is a required field. After you enter the basic information about an author and hit "Save", you will be prompted to indicated what that author created. If you are registering both musical compositions and sound recordings, you will need to check the box marked "Sound Recordings" and enter the author's contribution to the musical compositions in the box marked "Other."An author's contributions to a musical composition can be "Music," "Lyrics," or "Music and Lyrics." Fill in the appropriate information in the box marked "Other" for each author.

After you have entered the information for each author, all of the authors should be displayed on the main page:

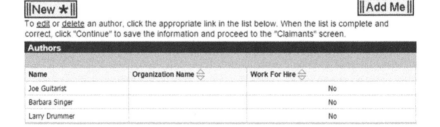

After you have completed all required fields, click the "Continue" button to be taken to the next page.

Claimants

For this section, you simply need to add the name and address for each claimant of the works being registered. In our example, the claimant is the

Chicago Commuters LLC because the rights in the compositions and sound recordings were transferred. When the claimant is not the author, eCO requires you to provide a transfer statement, which can be found at the bottom the page containing the fields for the claimant's information.

After you have completed all required fields, click the "Continue" button to be taken to the next page.

Limitation of Claim

You only need to complete this page if the works you are registering are based on previously registered material, previously published material, material in the public domain, or material not owned by the claimant. In other words, you should only worry about this section if the work you are registering is built upon a pre-existing work. The purpose of this section is to indicate to the Copyright Office that you are not attempting to claim copyright protection in a work that you did not create, or a work that is already protected. If this is the case for your works, you can find more information about how to complete this section by clicking on the "Material Excluded," "Previous Registration," and "New Material Included" links. After you have completed all required fields, click the "Continue" button to be taken to the next page.

Rights & Permissions

Enter the contact information for the person or entity to be contacted regarding copyright management information or permission to use the works being registered. After you have completed all required fields, click the "Continue" button to be taken to the next page.

Correspondent

Enter the contact information for the person or entity to be contacted by the Copyright Office if it has questions about the application. After you have completed all required fields, click the "Continue" button to be taken to the next page.

Mail Certificate

Enter the contact information for the person or entity to whom the copyright registration certificate should be mailed. After you have completed all required fields, click the "Continue" button to be taken to the next page.

Special Handling

If for some reason you need your application to be processed faster than normal, you can indicate that your application requires Special Handling. It should be noted that Special Handling is only available for a limited number of reasons and carries a hefty fee (currently $800). If you think that you may need Special Handling, you should consult with an attorney. After you have completed all required fields, click the "Continue" button to be taken to the next page.

Certification

Here, you are certifying that you are permitted by the author and/or the claimant to file the application and that everything contained in the application is true and correct. After you have completed all required fields, click the "Continue" button to be taken to the next page.

Fee and Deposit

You have now completed the application form. You should review the application to make sure that all of the information is accurate. Once you are satisfied that all of the information is correct, click the "Add to Cart" button at the top of the screen. You will then see your cart, which will confirm the filing fee. Click on the "Checkout" button at the top of the screen. You will then be prompted to pay the filing fee by using either a Copyright Office Deposit Account or a credit card.

Once you have paid the filing fee, you will need to submit your work. For this, you need to upload a digital copy of your musical compositions or sound recordings. The Copyright Office only accepts certain file types, which can be seen in the following list:

Audio	.aif, .aiff (Audio Interchange File Format)
	.au (Audio File)
	.mid, .midi, .rmi (Musical Instrument Digital Interface)
	.mp3 (MP3 Audio File or Layer 3 Audio Compression)
	.ra, .ram (Real Audio File)
	.rmi (Resource Interchangable File Format)
	.wav (Windows Wave Sound File)
	.wma (Windows Media Audio File)

Once you have uploaded your file in an acceptable format, you can submit your work and complete your application. You should receive an email confirming that your application is complete.

Registering by Mail

If you prefer to register by mail, you may also download and print the blank form (Form PA for musical compositions, Form SR for sound recordings) and complete it by hand or on your computer, or request a blank form by mail. The $85 fee for basic registration by paper application is higher than the fee for online application due to the higher labor costs associated with processing claims submitted on paper. To complete a paper application, follow these simple steps:

(1) Go to copyright.gov;

(2) Click on "Forms";

(3) Fill in all the necessary information on your personal computer or by hand;

(4) Print the form;

(5) Sign the form; and

(6) Mail it with a check or money order for $85 and your deposit (the physical copy of your work) to:

U.S. Copyright Office
101 Independence Avenue SE
Washington, D.C. 20559

After you have completed the necessary forms and submitted them, the Copyright Office will issue you a registration certificate if it accepts your application. In this certificate, the effective date of registration will be the date the Copyright Office received all required elements in acceptable form. Even if the Office takes a long time to process your application and mail your certificate, the effective date of registration will remain the date on which all of your application elements were received. In terms of the amount of time the Copyright Office takes to process your application, this will vary. However, it is crucial to note that the fastest option is to register online.

Chapter 5

How Do We Make Money With Our Music?

The music industry, despite all of its recent struggles, is still a huge, multi-billion dollar industry, and it is much more than simply a record industry. Rather, revenue comes from sources such as public performance royalties; licensing for uses in media such as movies, commercials, television, and video games; touring; and merchandising. Keep in mind what we discussed in Chapter 3: There are two distinct copyrights in a song—the composition copyright and the sound recording copyright, each of which confers different rights to the owner of the copyright. Composition copyrights give the owner the exclusive right to reproduce and distribute the work, prepare derivative works, and publicly perform the work. The right to reproduce and distribute would include the right to use the song in television programs, movies, commercials, and to make recordings of the song and distribute them via CD or digital download. The right to prepare derivative works would include the rights to act out the song in another medium (television or movie) and to synch the song with video to create an audiovisual work. Lastly, the right to publicly perform the work is very broad and would cover any performance of the song to a group larger than a gathering of friends and family (e.g., at a bar, restaurant, or concert venue or through digital streaming and radio broadcast). Even though these rights are broad, as discussed in the next chapter, there are some exceptions, including statutorily-mandated compulsory licenses.

Sound recording copyrights, on the other hand, come with far fewer rights. Such owners only have the exclusive right to directly or indirectly recapture actual sounds; prepare a derivative work in which actual sounds in the sound recording are rearranged, remixed, or otherwise altered in sequence or quality;

and publicly perform the work by means of digital audio transmission. In other words, sound recording copyrights would cover the right to synch the recording with video or make remixes of the recording itself but would not prevent others from duplicating the sound of the sound recording. Further, the public performance right for a sound recording is limited to digital audio transmissions such as streaming and does not cover radio broadcasts. As discussed in the next chapter, these rights may be even further limited in certain circumstances.

This chapter explores how your band can earn money from these copyrights and looks at some basic legal issues to consider when touring or selling merchandise.

Getting Paid for Your Compositions

As explained in previous chapters, the musical compositions may be the most valuable part of your song. Unlike performers, songwriters get royalties when their composition is played on the radio, whether it be the version of the composition they record or a recording by another band or musician. Even if the composition has languished in obscurity for decades and was only popular because another band covered it years later, the songwriter will receive royalties. But the owners of the sound recordings don't get a cent when a recording is played on the radio.

And one song can mean millions of dollars. Take the 2007 hit pop song "Umbrella" recorded by Rihanna. She may have made millions of dollars from it. But so did the songwriters. Terius Nash, a.k.a. The-Dream, is an Atlanta-based artist who co-wrote "Umbrella." In 2012, he claimed he had made about $15 million from the composition. Rihanna is a superstar and a household name. But The-Dream? Not so much, but he sure appears to have done well for himself (at least he claims) from this one composition.

This enormous revenue potential for your compositions is why it is vital to determine song-writing credits with your bandmates before recording and releasing an album or entering into a recording deal.

Below, we explore the most common revenue streams from compositions, including those from album sales, compulsory mechanical licenses from cover versions, public performance royalties, and other common licenses.

Mechanical License Royalties

Album Sales/Downloads

Owners of the composition copyright are typically paid royalties when recordings of their compositions are sold, even when they are one of the performers. Additionally, as explained below, once a recording of a composition is made, all other artists are entitled to create and sell recordings of that composition, provided they pay the compulsory mechanical license fee of 9.1 cents per copy. The issue here is how quickly 9.1 cents per composition sold can add up. If you wrote 10 compositions, recorded them on an album, and assigned these sound recordings to your record company, each physical or downloaded album sold by your record company can result in you getting 91 cents in mechanical license royalties from each sale, in addition to your sound recording royalties. The royalty increases if the composition is more than five minutes to 1.75 cents per minute (e.g., a royalty for a six-minute song would be 10.5 cents). The same math applies to compulsory mechanical royalties for covers. If you have a hit album or even just a hit song, this can create a significant revenue stream which can extend years into the future.

A songwriter and a record label can agree, however, to a rate lower than 9.1 cents per composition, and record companies may sometimes demand such lower rates as part of a record deal. And if you are signed to a publishing company, you may have to split these royalties with your publisher at the agreed-upon rate in your songwriter agreement. But, you should enter into any deal involving your compositions with a publishing company or record label cautiously, and if you have questions, make sure to consult an attorney or other expert in the field. As explained in Chapter 6, having your compositions registered with the Harry Fox Agency will help to ensure that you get paid the proper mechanical license royalties.

<u>Ring Tones</u>

Copies of compositions on a CD or sold as digital downloads are not the only area where you can receive mechanical license royalties. Royalties for ringtones can be lucrative, and the royalty rate is currently 24 cents per ringtone sold. So, again, if you have a hit composition, these can add up quickly.

<u>Streaming Services</u>

In addition, there are statutory mechanical royalties for your compositions when they are reproduced and used in connection with non-interactive, non-exempt digital audio transmission such as streaming services. For example, every time a composition is streamed on Spotify, in addition to Spotify paying a performance rights organization such as ASCAP or BMI for a public performance license for this composition, it has to pay a compulsory mechanical royalty for the composition. The Harry Fox Agency, in addition to administering mechanical licenses for cover versions of your compositions when you register your compositions with them, also issues and collects royalties for these streaming service mechanical licenses. And these licenses are relatively new to the music industry, having been established in late 2008.

Public Performance Royalties

You also have the right to receive a royalty every time a recording of your composition is played on the radio; through a digital service such as Pandora, YouTube, or Spotify; on stage by a band; in a restaurant, store or nightclub over certain stereo systems; or in other public settings. But, of course, you cannot be at all of these places at the same time, and there would be no reasonable way for you to determine your public performance royalties on your own. This is where performance rights organizations ("PROs") step in. They help to ensure that songwriters and publishers are paid royalties based on how frequently their compositions are played in public. In the United States, there are three primary PROs administering public performance royalties—ASCAP, BMI, and SESAC.

Choosing a PRO is an important step to take for any band that writes its own compositions. Without PRO affiliation you may not be taken as seriously when you submit your recordings to radio stations, as the radio station most likely will not negotiate directly with you for a public performance license. And a band cannot receive royalty revenue for digital music services such as Pandora or Spotify, because, again, they will most likely not even play your compositions if they are not registered with a PRO. Without registering with a PRO, you will not recover royalties for public performances of cover versions of your compositions.

In addition, ASCAP, BMI, and SESAC have entered into a joint venture that includes all the songs in their catalogs in something called the Jukebox License Agreement. This license, administered by the Nashville-based Jukebox License Office, gives the operator of a jukebox (such as a bar or restaurant) permission to play on this jukebox any song in the ASCAP, BMI, and SESAC catalogs. In short, if a band is serious about its music career, it must become affiliated with a PRO. Otherwise, you are leaving money on the table.

American Society of Composers, Authors, and Publishers (ASCAP)

ASCAP is the oldest PRO, founded in 1914. According to its website, it is the only American PRO created and controlled entirely by composers, writers, and publishers. Its client roster includes more than 585,000 members. The sign-up fee is $50, and royalty distributions occur quarterly. In 2015, it distributed approximately $867.4 million in public performance royalties to songwriters.

Broadcast Music, Inc. (BMI)

BMI was founded by radio broadcasters in 1939 as a reaction to the ASCAP monopoly in this field. Its client roster includes more than 750,000 members. There is no sign-up fee for songwriters. Royalty distributions occur quarterly if the distribution amount exceeds $2. Amounts owed that total less than $2 get rolled over to the following quarter. In the fiscal year that ended in June 2016, BMI distributed approximately $931 million in royalties to its members.

SESAC, Inc. (SESAC)

SESAC originally served European artists whose music was being performed in the United States. It now also serves U.S. artists. It is unique in that a songwriter cannot register to become a member. Instead, SESAC hand-picks particular songwriters with which it wants to work. It claims that this creates stronger relationships with clients than the other PROs. Its membership is not nearly as large as ASCAP's or BMI's, but it does boast hugely successful songwriters, most notably, Bob Dylan.

Other Licenses for Your Compositions

The compulsory mechanical license applies only to someone making and distributing recordings of your compositions. No such compulsory license exists to use your compositions for derivative works. Licenses come in many various names, and can cover a wide range of uses for your compositions. Here are two of the more common licenses.

Synchronization license

Someone may want to use your composition as background music in a movie, commercial, or video game. Using a composition in such a manner requires a license, commonly referred to as a synchronization license, for the uses listed. For example, it cost Cadillac a lot of money to use Led Zeppelin's "Rock And Roll," or for Nike to use The Beatles' "Revolution," which required a Lennon-McCartney songwriting credit in its television commercials.

There are complicated issues involved in such licenses for uses of your compositions in a film, commercial, television show, etc.—such as the term, geographic scope, use in different versions or derivative works, and so forth. And these licenses can be potentially lucrative. In order not to leave money on the table or give up more rights to your music than you should, it would be prudent to work with an attorney in negotiating and drafting such a license.

Print license

If your compositions become popular, a publisher may want to make sheet music of them, perhaps to distribute to beginning piano students or as part of a songbook for professional performers. These can become lucrative if, for example, print music is made for choirs, school bands, marching bands, piano students, and so forth.

Getting Help With Your Licensing

Signing with a traditional publisher can be a great option for songwriters, as the right publisher can help give you financial security and keep you doing what you love—writing music. However, most music recorded today does not get the attention of publishers. Plus, when publishers do find you, they will ask for a percentage of or all of your copyright ownership. Of course, it can be worth it to grant them the copyrights, because they might be offering a good deal of money for them. But you will lose control of your works.

Traditional publishers actively promote your compositions. They try to land you synchronization deals with commercial brands. They recommend your compositions as cover material for recording artists, and they facilitate co-writing between you and other songwriters.

Stepping into the space traditionally occupied by traditional publishers is the music licensing company, a sort of clearinghouse for music that is available for commercial licensing. These companies have thrived in the digital market, where search catalog features have made them a viable option for music supervisors and creative directors on all sorts of media projects. These services undercut the traditional publishers by attempting to offer music at lower fees to parties interested in using music commercially.

A common model followed by Music Dealers and Audiosocket is as follows:

(1) A songwriter writes and records a song;

(2) The songwriter submits her song to the licensing company;

(3) The licensing company reviews the submitted song;

(4) The licensing company either rejects the song or catalogs it—tagging by genre, instrumentation, etc.;

(5) A client of the licensing company (*e.g.,* Coca-Cola, Audi, or any other business) comes to the licensing company with a music licensing need;

(6) The licensing company supplies them with the song in the catalog and negotiates a price for the song; and

(7) The licensing company splits the upfront licensing fee with the songwriter (usually 50-50).

Licensing deals made through these services are usually non-exclusive (in fact, all of those from Music Dealers are), which means the artist whose composition is licensed maintains the right to license the composition elsewhere or use the composition in any other capacity, even while the composition is licensed out to the client. The deals may also be pre-approved, meaning the licensing company has the right to license a songwriter's compositions without special approval from the songwriter for the specific use. This arrangement can cause friction, but exists so that the licensing company can provide music licenses to clients with a quick turnaround.

In the case of Audiosocket, if the client requests an exclusive license, Audiosocket will ask the songwriter for approval. But all non-exclusive licenses are pre-approved to make the process smoother. Exclusivity in this context means that a client has the sole right to license the composition (probably during the term of the licensing deal, but perhaps for longer). Exclusive deals should come at a higher cost than non-exclusive deals.

If you are considering affiliating with a licensing company of this sort, we advise you to have an attorney look over the artist agreement before you sign it.

Getting Paid for Your Sound Recordings

The revenue streams for sound recordings are significantly different than those from compositions. This section addresses the common revenue streams, including selling your recordings, digital streaming public performance royalties, and master use licenses.

Selling Your Sound Recordings

This seems like an antiquated concept, selling your recordings. But after years of declining sales, in 2012 the U.S. recording industry actually saw an increase in sales. This increase was not on account of more CDs being sold. In fact, the sale of physical products decreased by 13 percent. Rather, the inevitable digitization of the record industry continued to march forward, as the sale of digital albums, singles, music videos, and digital tracks rose 14 percent, to approximately 1.66 billion units. So, a discussion on selling recordings of your music should start with digital downloads.

Digital downloads have marked a revolution in music consumption. By digital downloads, we mean Internet-based music stores that sell MP3s and other digital music formats. iTunes is the dominant such store. However, Amazon.com, Google, and others offer digital download sales. Further, Rhapsody, Pandora, and other streaming services offer the ability to buy and download music.

The Eminem Conundrum: Is a Sound Recording Download a Sale or a License?

Sometimes, the least likely artists become pioneers in music law. Take Eminem. The controversial rapper signed over the rights to his recordings to his production company in 1995, well before a digital download industry existed. In 1998, Eminem was signed to Aftermath Entertainment, a subsidiary of the major label Universal Music Group. These contracts from the late 1990s were silent about how the label would calculate royalties for digital downloads. But as Slim Shady rose in popularity, the digital download industry was born, iTunes emerged, and soon it became a major profit center.

How digital downloads would be calculated became a major issue, as Eminem's production company would receive between 12 percent to 20 percent of the adjusted retail price for a full record sold, but would receive 50 percent of Aftermath's net receipts for the licensing revenue for the sound recordings. Eminem argued digital downloads were licenses, and he should receive 50 percent of what Aftermath received from the likes of Apple for sales of these downloads. The label, of course, argued they were sales of albums. After a long court battle, the appellate court in 2010 ruled in favor of Eminem, and found that digital downloads were licenses. However, as the parties were fighting over damages, in 2012 they settled, the terms of which are confidential. However, other artists, such as James Taylor and the Temptations, have brought similar suits.

Today, recording contracts classify digital downloads as album sales, so these issues generally apply only to recording contracts for established artists. But this case is a good example of the new frontiers (and uncertainty) for revenues in relation to digital music.

If you are signed to a record label, it should have deals in place with these on-line retailers. And when you are looking for a recording contract and negotiating with a record label, you should ask about what sort of digital distribution the label has in place.

The digital landscape has also democratized music retail. Where it used to be next to impossible for an independent artist or small label to get positioning or shelf space for an album, the sheer breadth of the digital marketplace allows independent artists to have a presence in digital stores. However, these stores still do not just sell any artist's music. To help independent artists get their music sold in the digital marketplace, digital aggregators have emerged. Digital aggregators are intermediary service providers that distribute your recordings to digital marketplaces. If you are an unsigned, independent band, you should consider signing with an aggregator such as TuneCore, CD Baby, Nimbit, ReverbNation, INgrooves, The Orchard, or Redeye.

Brick-and-mortar sales can be lucrative if your records are being produced and distributed by a major label. Also, some of the companies that help with independent digital distribution can also help get your physical albums into brick-and-mortar stores. An independent band may also consign CDs at local record stores, and of course can sell music through its website or at live shows.

Sound Recordings On The Air: Digital Streaming vs. Radio

Interactive Streaming Services

When your recordings are streamed through on-demand ("interactive") music listening services like Rhapsody or Spotify, you are entitled to money for those plays—the more plays, the more money. No compulsory license exists for these services, so they have to negotiate with record labels and other owners of sound recordings to have the rights to play these recordings. What you are paid is dependent on many factors. If you are signed to a record label, the label is paid by the streaming service first, and then distributes your share afterward. If you are unsigned, but using a digital aggregator like TuneCore or CD Baby, the digital aggregator may take its cut of revenue before passing the rest along to you.

It is practically impossible to get your music on an interactive service all by yourself. Major labels lobby for rates for their artists. Indie labels come together to negotiate on behalf of indie artists. Completely unaffiliated artists have no one to negotiate for them, and digital aggregators do not negotiate individual rates with unknown acts. After all, it is highly unlikely that any completely independent artist commands a fan base so large that a music service like Spotify cannot live without it.

Non-Interactive Streaming Services: Digital Performance Royalties

Non-interactive digital transmissions include satellite radio (like Sirius-XM), Internet radio, services like Pandora, and cable music channels. Recording artists (anyone whose performance is embodied on a sound recording) are owed a royalty for non-interactive digital transmissions of commercially released sound recordings. This is actually a compulsory license that allows these services to stream these songs, but at a cost. This is different than the public performance license for the compositions—which these services have to pay as well.

Even though a Pandora user gets to choose the genre of music he wants to listen to, he cannot actually choose a particular song; therefore, it is a non-interactive—sometimes called passive—service. These royalties are known as digital performance royalties, and they are administered by a not-for-profit performance rights organization called SoundExchange. While there are several PROs collecting royalties for public performances on behalf of songwriters, SoundExchange is the only PRO collecting digital streaming royalties for sound recordings on behalf of recording artists.

The Copyright Royalty Board sets the rate to be paid to Sound-Exchange by the various entities required to pay digital sound recording performance royalties. SoundExchange distributes 50% of royalties to the owner of the sound recording, 45% to the principal recording artists, and 5% to session musicians whose performances are featured on the recording. Notice the advantage of being both the owner and principal artist featured on a sound recording. If you are both, you get 95% of SoundExchange's royalties. And this is not an insignificant amount of money. For example, in 2015 SoundExchange distributed approximately $802.6 million in royalties. A sound recording can be registered with SoundExchange at its website, soundexchange.com.

What about radio?

Regular terrestrial AM and FM radio is an area in which recording artists do not control the uses of their recordings. As explained above, radio stations must secure public performance licenses from the owners of the compositions that they play over their airwaves, and most composers license the right to grant public performance licenses to PROs. Therefore, radio stations obtain licenses from these entities to play *compositions*. However, radio stations do not have to secure any licenses to the *sound recordings*. This is because under the Copyright Act, the owner of a sound recording does not own an exclusive right to the public performance of their recordings, except for the right to digital audio transmissions.

Using the argument that analog or terrestrial radio play generates sales of recordings, the radio industry has effectively lobbied to maintain the status quo in copyright law, so that it does not have to pay anything to broadcast a sound recording over the air.

There have been numerous hearings before Congress that have addressed this issue. For example, on June 6, 2012, the "Future of Audio" Congressional Subcommittee Hearing featured testimony from the likes of Cary Sherman from the Recording Industry Association of America and jazz bassist Ben Allison, both of whom advocated for establishing a licensing system for terrestrial radio stations to perform sound recordings.

Non-Compulsory Licensing for Your Recordings

Master Use Licenses

Licensing is an excellent way to monetize a sound recording. Today, if such a license is given to the producer of a movie, TV show, TV advertisement, corporate presentation, or any other audio-visual work, such a license is called a master use license. The sound recording owner is allowing the producer to literally synch the music to the production. This is the equivalent of the synchronization license discussed above for a composition.

There is no such thing as a compulsory master use license, so the party interested in obtaining rights for a sound recording must persuade the owner of a sound recording to grant it these rights. Thus, the owner of a sound recording is in a powerful bargaining position. The licensee's project cannot be completed until the licensor approves the proposed use by the licensee. This approval could be entirely contingent on the amount of money offered by the licensee, or it could hinge on other factors as well. For example, the licensor could reject a reasonable fee if the message of the licensee's project is fundamentally at odds with the licensor's moral convictions.

Though the owner of a sound recording is in a powerful bargaining position as to the recordings that he or she owns, there are so many recordings out there that—more likely than not—a potential licensee can find another song to adequately replace yours if you do not agree to the terms set forth in the master use license. The potential licensee could also simply hire another band to record the composition, and in doing so would need only a license to use the composition.

There are many ways a recording artist can increase the likelihood that her recordings will get licensed. The standard way is to sign a deal with a record label that guarantees (1) that the label will actively pursue licensing opportunities for the artist's recordings, and (2) that the profits from licenses will be split between the label and the artist. Today, there are ways for unsigned recording artists to generate licensing revenue through intermediate licensing companies such as Audiosocket, Music Dealers, and other companies that specialize in licensing music. The fees generated through these services can be a nice revenue stream for independent artists. However, they are likely less per transaction than a label would negotiate for a signed artist.

Composition Royalties: Follow Your Money

Understanding licensing basics is essential to navigating the potential revenue streams for your compositions.

Your Composition

Mechanical Licenses

A statutory license set at 9.1 cents per song sold, paid by a record label to the composer and/or publisher. The Harry Fox Agency generally administers and pays the compulsory license for cover versions of compositions, as well as for ringtones and streaming services.

Other Licenses

Synchronization
(e.g., films, video games, commercials)

Print
(e.g., sheet music, scores)

Collected by the songwriter (if she does not have a publisher), or by a publishing administrator or music licensing company negotiating such licenses on behalf of the songwriter.

Public Performance

(e.g., radio, live performances, digital music services)

ASCAP   BMI   SESAC

Collected by performance rights organizations ("PROs") when your songs are performed in public. 50 percent goes to the writer(s) of the songs, and 50 percent goes to the publisher(s) of the songs.

Sound Recording Royalties: Follow Your Money

The same licensing basics are essential to navigating the potential revenue streams for your sound recordings.

Your Recording

Album Sales

The royalty rate that your band has negotiated with its record label; typically received after the label has fully recouped its advance.

Master Use License
(*e.g., films, video games, commercials*)

Collected by the owner of the sound recording (e.g., the band or record label), and negotiated for any particular use.

Digital Streaming Public Performance

SoundExchange

For play on services like Internet radio and streaming services. Split is 50% of royalties to the owner of the sound recording, 45% to the principal recording artist featured, and 5% between session musicians whose performances are featured on the recording.

Recording Device Royalties

As you can see, if your band does not write its own music (or if you are not one of the composers), a substantial portion of your income will be tied to records sales and downloads. This is why so many musicians feel so strongly about illegal downloading and file sharing sites (Napster, Aimster, Grokster). The Recording Industry Association of America has put in a tremendous amount of effort to curtail illegal copying of music. And the U.S. Congress took action to lessen the impact of illegal copying by enacting the Audio Home Recording Act in 1992. The Act was a compromise between technology manufacturers and the record industry to allow companies to manufacture and sell devices that enable consumers to record or copy sound recordings.

The Act requires manufacturers of recording devices and recording media (CDRs) to pay a royalty to the Copyright Office. The royalty for recording devices equates to 2% of the price of each device, but not less than $1 or more than $12, with the maximum depending on the design of the device; for recording media, the royalty is 3% of the price. The Copyright Office divides the royalties received into two funds: the Sound Recordings Fund and the Musical Works Fund. Sixty percent of the revenue is deposited into the Sound Recordings Fund, and forty percent into the Musical Works Fund. The royalties deposited into the Sound Recordings Fund is distributed by the Alliance of Artists and Recording Companies based upon digital and retail sales, with 58 percent being distributed to the owner of the copyright in the sound recording, 38 percent being distributed to the featured artists, and 4 percent being distributed to non-featured artists and vocalists. The royalties deposited into the Musical Works Fund are split evenly between writers and publishers. Pursuant to an agreement with their members, ASCAP, BMI and SESAC apply for and distribute money to their writers, and Harry Fox applies for and distributes money to its publishers. Again, however, writers and publishers who are not members of these organizations can still file claims for royalties on their own. Unfortunately, perhaps because the exemptions and exceptions provided for under the Act are so broad, the Copyright Office only distributes about $1.5 million annually.

Touring and Merchandise

Touring can mean long hours driving, bad hotels, even worse food, inconsistent venues, crooked club owners . . . and the experience of a lifetime as you coalesce as a group and bring your act to audiences outside of your home town. We are not attempting with this book to provide business advice on how to tour. And as you probably know from experience, touring is certainly not a guaranteed source of revenue. In fact, bands often lose money on their tours, yet they hit the road to promote their music and simply to perform.

But touring can often involve contracts with venues, and you should make sure that several clauses are clear in any such contract:

(1) **Payment:** Do you get part or all of the door? Do you get a set fee? Is there a minimum number of people who have to attend the show or purchase tickets for you to get paid? Are there any expenses that the venue can recoup before paying you? Can the venue get a cut of your merchandise or charge you to sell merchandise? These are all issues to consider when reviewing your contract.

(2) **Rider:** Make sure that you specify issues such as sound equipment your band will need (or even gear, such as a piano), whether you can sell merchandise, the food and drinks the venue will provide, and whether you get to have a guest list for free tickets to the show for your friends, family, the press, etc.

(3) **Promotion:** What are the venue's obligations to promote your show, and what are your obligations to promote the show?

(4) **Exclusivity:** If you play this gig, when can you come back to the area and perform again? Contracts often have geographic exclusivity for a certain period of time to help ensure that there is demand for the gig. After all, if you'll be playing down the street in a week, this could affect ticket sales for both shows.

(5) **Breaking the contract**: What happens if you cannot make the gig, such as your van breaking down, your lead singer breaking

her leg, or the band breaking up? Try to limit or remove any liability if you have a legitimate reason for not making the gig. Of course, if you just do not show up, then you could be on the hook for certain fees. But if you have no conceivable way of performing that night based on an "act of God" or other calamity, you should not also have to suffer economic consequences.

Of course, there could be multiple other clauses in a contract, and you should carefully read and consider all of these. Also, if a venue refuses to enter into a contract with you, this may give you reason to consider not taking this gig, and finding a potential show at another venue with more transparent and official business practices.

As mentioned above, touring gives you an opportunity to sell some CDs, T-shirts, posters, and other merchandise. And you can always sell merchandise from your website or through a site such as Bandcamp.

This book does not intend to provide you advice on how to run your merchandising program. However, you should be careful to obtain the necessary rights to use artwork in your merchandise. For example, if you have hired a photographer to shoot your album cover photo and promotional photos, and you want to use these photos on a poster or T-shirt, make sure you have obtained the rights to do so from the photographer. (For a more in-depth discussion of this, see Chapter 9.) If you have not acquired all rights for the images from the photographer, and merchandising rights are not included in your contract, you must attempt to acquire these rights before creating your merchandise. Otherwise, if you cannot get permission from the photographer, your sale of the merchandise may very well infringe his copyrights to the images.

In addition, make sure to keep track of your merchandise sales, both to distribute any revenue in accordance with your band's band agreement, as well as to make sure that you are in compliance with state and federal tax laws.

Eight Great Music Industry Web Resources to Help Your Music Business

A great way to help you earn a living with your music is to stay on top of the latest news and trends in the music industry, as well as to consult trusted resources with information and advice. The following eight websites provide such information.

- Future of Music Coalition
  futureofmusic.org
  The Future of Music Coalition is a nonprofit that serves many behind-the-scenes functions for the music community. They are a lobby for musicians in Washington, D.C., and a research center. They recently released an illuminating report called Artist Revenue Streams, which is designed to track changes in musicians' sources of income over time.

- DIY Musician
  diymusician.cdbaby.com
  Run by CD Baby, this blog goes above and beyond to help musicians (of course it may have a bit of CD Baby bias). The free musician guides alone are worth a peek—handbooks on such topics as how to tour, how to maximize social media tools, how to get on the radio, etc. In addition, the blog boasts videos for the weary reader.

- Music Think Tank
  musicthinktank.com
  MTT is Hypebot's music leg. The main Hypebot page is often relevant to musicians, and MTT is exclusively about music. In typical blog format you get an array of subjects covered by a large network of practicing independent musicians or music business people.

- TuneCorner
  blog.tunecore.com
  Run by TuneCore, this blog—like DIY Musician—may be biased but it is excellent. It features educational video clips and insightful articles, mostly on the topic of getting paid for one's music.

- Unified Manufacturing
unifiedmanufacturing.com/blog
Unified Manufacturing provides excellent CD wholesaling services. They also run this really great blog. The focus is on promotions and the best packaging practices. But they branch out to more wide-ranging discussion topics as well, like how to maximize a monthly newsletter and the causes of band squabbles.

- Artists House
artistshousemusic.org
Artists House is a wonderful nonprofit organization, and much of the work it does gets put up on the website. There are hours of video clips to watch, which often serve as tutorials for independent musicians. Videos and articles are divided into practical categories like marketing, production, music business, legal, and careers in music.

- Brabec & Brabec
musicandmoney.com
Run by twin brothers with extensive industry experience, primarily on the publishing side of things. This site is mostly in service to their book, *Music, Money And Success*, now in its 7th edition. But the site also includes articles offering practical advice on discrete topics such as movie scores and pre-cleared compositions.

- Lefsetz Letter
lefsetz.com/wordpress
Bob Lefsetz has been enthralled with music forever, and has carved out a niche for himself in the business as an irreverent and principled critic and commentator. He is widely read within the industry, has an entertaining writing style, and is insightful.

Chapter 6

Can We Use Other People's Music
(And When Can Other People Use Ours)?

You may feel like your compositions and recordings are your "babies," and you may want to prevent these songs from being used by other artists. This is not always possible. In this chapter, we address three primary ways musicians can use other artists' music generally without their permission: cover versions, parodies, and sampling which could be considered a fair or de minimis use.

Cover Versions

Songs can assume new identities in the hands of other artists. You only need to watch The Voice to hear how the same song can sound so different, sometimes better, sometimes worse, when performed by a different artist. Or take how Jimi Hendrix transformed Bob Dylan's acoustic gem "All Along The Watchtower" into a high-octane electric guitar workout. Or how Metallica turned Bob Seger's "Turn The Page" into a heavy metal anthem and Beyoncé put an R&B twist on Billy Joel's "Honesty." Jazz artists routinely record standards from the Great American Songbook or from other jazz composers and rework the songs, putting their personal touches on the music.

To record these cover versions, the musicians needed permission from the composers of these compositions, right? Well, the answer is actually no. A musician can cover a composition without getting permission from the composer. As long as the cover version does not change "the basic melody or fundamental character of the work" (to quote the Copyright Act), copyright law offers something called a compulsory "mechanical license," which allows anyone who follows the procedures associated with getting the mechanical license to record a composition that has previously been recorded and distributed in the United States.

So if your band wants to record a cover version of a composition for a new album, you need to obtain a mechanical license from the entity that owns the copyright in the composition. A few simple rules exist to get this license. First, as stated above, the cover has to retain the basic melody and character of the composition. Next, you have to provide notice to the owner of the copyrighted composition that you are recording a cover version of the composition within 30 days after making the recording and prior to distributing it. After that, you are free to distribute hard copies or digital copies of the composition, and pay a royalty rate of 9.1 cents per composition or 1.75 cents per minute of playing time or fraction thereof (this applies for songs longer than five minutes) for each copy of the song sold, whichever is greater. This royalty rate is set by the Copyright Royalty Board, and increases from time to time. So, if you were to press 1,000 CDs of an album that includes two cover compositions, each less than five minutes long, you would owe mechanical royalties of $182 (9.1 cents x two compositions x 1,000 CDs).

The mechanical royalty rate is the same for digital permanent downloads (oftentimes referred to as "DPDs"), such as those sold through iTunes. So, if your album includes two covers, each less than five minutes long, and the compositions were each downloaded 1,000 times, you would owe the same royalties of $182. Note that you owe the owner of the original composition mechanical royalties even for cover recordings that you give away for free.

This compulsory mechanical licensing system helps foster musical creativity through the exploration and expansion of compositions, as the license comes with the authority to create a new arrangement of the work. No bright-line rules exist as to how much a band can alter an arrangement in a recording and still qualify for a compulsory license. A good "sound check" may be to consider if a judge with little or no musical training or knowledge, when listening to the song as part of a copyright infringement case, could still recognize that the cover is the same composition.

The converse is true as well: If another musician wants to cover your compositions, they just have to get this license. This process provides a fair compensation for the composers. So if you have recorded and distributed your original music, you cannot stop an artist from re-recording your composition and releasing a cover version of it, as long as the artist who records your composition complies with the rules set forth in copyright law.

For example, if an artist has recorded and is distributing a cover version of your composition, or a song that is substantially similar to your song, and has not provided you with notice that they intended to do so, they never obtained a mechanical license. You have the right to send them a cease-and-desist letter to demand that they stop selling and distributing the composition, or demand that they obtain a license. In addition, you may have a potential copyright infringement action against this artist. However, if the artist has complied with the relatively straightforward rules to obtain a compulsory mechanical license, think of the cover version as publicity for your composition, and a potential revenue stream that did not require much work from you.

Mechanical Licensor—The Harry Fox Agency

The Harry Fox Agency has emerged as the preeminent mechanical rights licensing agency. Both large and independent music publishers register their compositions with Harry Fox, which issues mechanical licenses and collects the royalties on behalf of the music publishers. If your compositions are licensed to a publisher, odds are that this publisher has registered your compositions with Harry Fox.

If you want to cover a composition, you should first check with Harry Fox (harryfox.com) to see if the composition is in Harry Fox's catalog. Harry Fox allows musicians to search the songwriter and publisher information for a particular composition on its website's "Songfile" service, with the option to purchase mechanical licenses online. A more recent service called Lime-light (songclearance.com) has also emerged to serve independent musicians in obtaining mechanical licenses. A musician can enter in the artist name and title of the composition he wishes to license, and Limelight will research the copyright status of the composition, obtain a license on the musician's behalf, and provide a .pdf copy of the license within 10 to 15 business days. The service costs $15, plus the statutory royalties for the number of CDs or downloads licensed (again, 9.1 cents per unit for compositions under five minutes long).

A number of other websites exist that allow musicians to search for the copyright holder of a composition. A good starting place is the U.S. Copyright Office's website (copyright.gov), which contains a searchable record of copyrighted materials. ASCAP, BMI, and SESAC also have searchable databases on their websites. Finally, copyright information is likely printed on the original artist's CD, or wherever the music is distributed.

Most likely, the composition will be in the Harry Fox catalog, and you can notify Harry Fox of your intent to cover that composition. Also, if you run your own publishing company—a company that controls your compositions and collects your royalties for your compositions—you can register your compositions with Harry Fox. As long as your publishing company has had at least one composition from its catalog released commercially as a sound recording by a third party—i.e., a record label—within the last 12 months, you can register as a Harry Fox affiliate. When this occurs, Harry Fox will manage the mechanical licensing for your compositions. Simply put, registering your compositions with Harry Fox could help open up potential revenue streams for your music, and will streamline the compulsory mechanical rights process for your compositions if other musicians want to cover them.

When a Cover Does Not Qualify for a Compulsory License

Instances exist when a new version of a song would not be eligible for a compulsory mechanical license. Remember the language in the Copyright Act: the cover must not change "the basic melody or fundamental character of the work." Accordingly, if your band just uses the lyrics of another artist's composition and puts them over a completely different melody and arrangement, writes entirely new lyrics and uses them with a copyrighted composition, or just uses a small but identifiable and important part of another artist's composition, then you would have to negotiate a license with the owner of the composition. No standard licensing rate would exist for such a license, so the composition owner would be able to set the rate they wish for this license. And if you do not agree to this rate, then you cannot obtain the license.

Using Compositions Without Acquiring a License Can Be Costly!

Recently, Robin Thicke and Pharrell Williams were sued for Infringing Marvin Gaye's composition, "Got To Give It Up." A California jury finding the works were substantially similar awarded Marvin Gaye's estate $7.4 million in damages.

Similarly, the melody in Coldplay's Grammy-winning Song of the Year, "Viva La Vida," struck a chord with guitar icon Joe Satriani when he first heard it in 2008. Satriani sued Coldplay for copyright infringement, claiming that substantial original portions of his composition "If I Could Fly," written and recorded in 2004, were used without permission by Coldplay in "Viva La Vida." The suit was settled outside of court, and under the terms of the dismissal, Coldplay did not have to admit any wrongdoing. The financial terms of the settlement have not been publicly disclosed. Although a court never decided the legal infringement issue, side-by-side comparisons of the two recordings available on YouTube have allowed millions of listeners to decide for themselves whether Coldplay actually copied Satriani's composition. Despite the fact that Coldplay settled this dispute outside of court, it may have paid a high price for the alleged infringement.

Fair Use Exception: Parodies

For the reasons discussed above, a new composition may sometimes include part of another musician's composition and not qualify for a compulsory mechanical license because it does not retain the basic melody or character of the composition. However, times exist when such a new composition may not even need a mechanical license to be released on an album. This is because a fair use exception exists when a cover version of a composition can be considered a parody of the original.

A parody is a "fair use" of the composition if it is a new work that comments on an existing work. Think "Weird Al" Yankovic. He puts his own lyrics on compositions recorded by the likes of Michael Jackson and MC Hammer to Nirvana and Madonna and creates entirely new, humorous works. He could argue he does not need to get permission to create such compositions because he is creating parodies.

No bright-line rules exist as to what constitutes fair use, and courts analyze fair use on a case-by-case basis using the following factors:

- The purpose and character of the use (*e.g.*, whether for commercial or educational purposes);

- The nature of the copyrighted work (whether it is a work of fiction or non-fiction);

- The amount of the portion used in relation to the work as a whole; and

- The effect of the use on the potential market or value of the copyrighted work.

The Supreme Court has had an opportunity to address what constitutes a song parody. In the important 1994 decision *Campbell* v. *Acuff-Rose Music*, the Court found that the rap group 2 Live Crew's parody of Roy Orbison's classic "Oh, Pretty Woman" could be a fair use of the composition. In this case, 2 Live Crew's manager informed the publisher that controlled "Oh, Pretty Woman" that it was going to record and release a parody of the composition—similar to what "Weird Al" does—with comical and crass lyrics in place of Orbison's romantic and subdued lyrics. 2 Live Crew agreed that it could not receive a compulsory mechanical license for its version, because it altered the composition more than allowed by the Copyright Act. Not obligated to grant 2 Live Crew a license, Orbison's publisher denied this license to the composition.

Nevertheless, 2 Live Crew released the song "Pretty Woman," which became a hit on the group's 1989 album, *As Clean As They Wanna Be.*

This led to a copyright infringement lawsuit that made it all the way to the Supreme Court. The Court found that 2 Live Crew's version of "Pretty Woman" had sufficiently commented on Orbison's original such that it could possibly be considered a parody. The Court found that because the rap version was a substantial reworking of Orbison's composition, this new version "reasonably could be perceived as commenting on the original or criticizing it, to some degree. 2 Live Crew juxtaposes the romantic musings of a man whose fantasy comes true, with degrading taunts, a bawdy demand for sex, and a sigh of relief from paternal responsibility."

Sampling: Fair Use and De Minimis Exceptions

The above examples explored the ability to use another's composition. But, what about another's recordings? There are no compulsory licenses allowing someone to use another person's sound recording. In most cases, an artist cannot use your recording without a license. Thorny issues come up in the context of "sampling" an artist's sound recording. The safest route is to obtain permission from both the copyright owner of the sound recording and (depending upon how much is sampled) the underlying composition. License fees for sampling vary greatly depending on: (1) how much of the music is sampled; (2) the popularity of the music you intend to sample; and (3) the intended use of the sample in your recording (if your entire recording is based upon a sample it will be more costly than a minor use of the sample). Because no statutory royalty rates exist for samples (like the mechanical royalty for covers), the copyright owner can charge the artist whatever she wants for the use of the sample and can refuse to grant permission altogether. On the other hand, the sound recording copyright owner cannot prevent another artist from recreating the recording on her own. So, the cost of recreating another recording usually works to cap the sampling license fee.

There has been a lot of discussion about whether sampling should be considered a "fair use," and, as such, not require a license. Consider, for example, artists such as the DJ Girl Talk, who has created song "mashups" that combine numerous samples of recordings with original elements. These mashups may use the key melodic riffs and hooks of some of the most popular classic and current Top 40 hits. The sampling rates for these compositions and recordings would most likely be exorbitant and cost prohibitive. However, an argument exists that such uses of the samples are fair uses: by combining so many samples and other elements into a new song, the artist has "transformed" the samples into an entirely new work. This is not a settled or simple area of copyright law by any means. However, as digital technology advances and more artists innovate how to create digital music, this will be an area of law that develops through the courts and perhaps legislation.

Battle of the Bands: Sampling Issues—Cold Times in Creativity

A sample can make a song. The first few bars of Vanilla Ice's 1990 hit single "Ice Ice Baby" offer a prime example. It seems instantly catchy and memorable; the reason it seems so familiar, however, is because the tune is nearly identical to Queen and David Bowie's 1981 hit "Under Pressure." Queen and David Bowie sued Vanilla Ice for copyright infringement for sampling their beat without permission. Vanilla Ice settled the case out of court for an undisclosed amount, but speculation is that it was high. Following the settlement, Vanilla Ice followed all the proper legal procedures in licensing the samples, and "Ice Ice Baby" went on to be a huge hit.

Similarly, if only a small amount of a recording is used, that use may be considered a fair use. Courts have ruled that sampling even small and distorted portions of recordings is copyright infringement. For example, in *Bridgeport Music, Inc. v. Dimension Films*, the 6th Circuit found that the rap group N.W.A.'s use of a two-second, three-note guitar riff that was drastically altered from how it appeared on Funkadelic's "Get Off Your Ass And Jam" required a license. However, the 9th Circuit recently rejected this approach in

VMG Salsoul, LLC v. Ciccone and found that Madonna's use of a short "horn hit" sample in her song "Vogue" did not infringe the copyright in the sampled sound recording because it was a de minimis sampling. De minimis means that the average audience would not recognize that the sample was taken from the work of another. While these two cases highlight the confusion concerning the legality of sampling, Bridgeport is still good law in certain parts of the country and demonstrates that there is a risk in not getting a license from the owner of the sound recording and composition to sample a song in your recording.

Battle of the Bands:
The Beastie Boys and a Flute Sample

Hip-hop pioneers the Beastie Boys built many of their classics by laying their vocals over a bed of sampled recordings. To use these samples, the Beastie Boys would acquire licenses for the sound recording from the owner of these recordings, which was often an artist's record label. They did this to get a license to sample a short, six-second segment of flutist James Newton's recording of his composition "Choir" that they used in their hit "Pass The Mic" from the 1992 album *Check Your Head*. Although not widely known to the general public, Newton is considered among jazz fans as one of the world's premier jazz and avant-garde flutists, and his composition "Choir" appeared on an album Newton recorded for the jazz and classical record label ECM Records.

The Beastie Boys obtained a license from ECM to use a sample of the sound recording of Newton's "Choir" in "Pass The Mic." No dispute existed that Newton—as part of his recording deal with ECM—had licensed the **sound recordings** for "Choir" to ECM. This gave the record label the right to grant the Beastie Boys the license to sample a three-note portion of the sound recording in "Pass The Mic." The Beastie Boys, however, did not obtain a license from Newton to use **the composition** "Choir" in "Pass The Mic."

Newton filed a copyright infringement lawsuit in federal court in California. Newton claimed that while the Beastie Boys may have obtained the right to use the sound recording to "Choir," they did not have the right to use the composition. Interestingly, while no dispute existed that the Beastie Boys did not have a license to use the composition "Choir," the court ruled that the small, three-note segment of "Choir" the Beastie Boys used was not copyrightable because it was not creative enough to be copyrighted. As such, the Beastie Boys prevailed in court, and the judge ruled that they had not infringed the copyright to Newton's composition.

Chapter 7

What Do We Look for in a Recording Contract?

Everyone hopes for that elusive recording contract. But the fact is that you would be better off without one than entering into one of the type many burgeoning artists—and even some established artists—have signed. Often, after entering into a recording contract with a band, a record company does little to nothing for the band. Upon inspection of the recording contract, the band discovers the record company is actually not required to do anything. Such unfriendly contracts are a common reason why artists seek assistance from attorneys.

Generally, a recording contract is an agreement between artists and a record company where the artists agree to deliver to the record company a certain number of albums worth of recordings, and the record company obtains rights to those recordings (including the right to sell those recordings) and agrees to pay the artists a royalty for each album sold. Typically the artists receive an advance, which is recouped, along with all expenses incurred in production and marketing, out of the artists' royalty payments. Major items typically negotiated in a recording contract include the number of albums the artist is obligated to deliver, the amount of the advance and the royalty percentage paid to the artist upon sales, and control of the recordings after termination.

In this chapter, we review provisions often found in a recording contract, using an actual agreement entered into by one of our clients—a client that had already recorded five albums—as an example. There were provisions in this contract that clearly were unfair to the band, and we suggest alternate and more equitable provisions that you should endeavor to have in a recording contract. We cover only the primary provisions. Of course, there are many other clauses typically contained in a recording contract, and they are important as well.

A suggested approach to enter into a contract is to understand the provisions below and to try to come to a mutual understanding on them with the record company. But before executing any contract, you should hire an attorney familiar with recording contracts and get them involved in the process.

Services

Recording contracts typically have a provision that states the artist is being *exclusively* employed by the record company. This provision is intended to stop the artist from recording music with another record company during the term of the recording contract. Our example contract provided that the record company was engaging:

> Artist to render its exclusive audio and audio-visual services for Recording Company's benefit and for the benefit of Recording Company's licensees and distributors.

While this is a fairly standard provision, as explained earlier, this clause may result in the sound recordings being considered works-made-for-hire. Thus it could be interpreted to transfer to the record label the copyrights for any sound recordings created during the contract. As such, the life or duration of the copyright may be shorter than if the copyright were to be considered owned by the band and then assigned to the record label. Since, as explained below, it is often appropriate for the sound recording copyrights to revert to the band, characterizing the sound recordings as works-made-for-hire typically benefits neither the recording artist nor the record company.

Term

Recording contracts typically include a provision setting out the length, or term, of the agreement. Our example contract stated:

> Agreement shall remain in full force and effect . . . up to and

until eighteen (18) months following delivery, or twelve (12) months after street release, of the last album released under the Agreement. . . .

Recording Company's sound recording copyright interest in the Master Recordings Produced hereunder . . . shall survive termination of this Agreement.

The term in our example contract is fairly standard. Its impact is that if the record company does not exercise its option (described below) to require a subsequent album, the agreement will expire shortly after the release (18 months after delivery, 12 months after street release) of the first album. As such, the artist must understand that with a clause of this type, a record company can choose to walk away from the agreement after the first album. Of course, as shown below, unless the record company has some affirmative obligations under the agreement, this may not mean much. As for the survival clause (the last sentence of the provision set out above), we will discuss that below.

Master Recordings—Existing Masters

In the situation related to our example contract, the artist had already recorded five albums when the record company signed them. It is not uncommon in such a situation—especially when the old albums are going to be remixed and remastered, and are not already owned by another label—for a record company to require distribution rights in these sound recordings. Our example contract stated:

Artist has previously recorded Master Recordings as listed in Schedule A. . . . All rights to said Master Recordings including the sound recording copyrights in said Masters and the rights to reproduce the recordings . . . shall remain with Recording Company] for seven (7) years from the date of execution of this Agreement. Recording Company shall have one option to extend the term for an additional seven (7) years upon written notice to Artist and upon payment of $.25 per Album sold during the initial term of this Agreement, ***minus any unrecouped balance in Artist's royalty account.***

Here is where the contract really begins to unravel. Why should the record company get "all rights" to the sound recordings for albums it paid nothing to generate? If no records are sold during the initial term, the record company would be permitted to extend its rights to these works for an additional seven years, without paying a dime. Why should the record company be permitted to extend its rights to these works for an additional seven years if it was not able to sell a single record? Or for $.25, if it was able to sell only one?

A fair value for the exclusive rights to distribute these albums should be required to extend these distribution rights. And, while a reasonable argument exists that the fair value is best determined by looking at the number of albums sold in the prior term, this assumes that efforts to sell those albums took place. Many times, record companies obtain rights to these albums and do next to nothing to market and sell them, relying instead on the artist to do the marketing and selling (which many must do to put food on the table). Of course, if the artist had the expertise to market and sell albums, it would not have needed the record company in the first place. And, if the artist is doing all the work to market and sell the albums, why should they be required to share revenue with the record company?

Master Recordings—New Masters

Recording contracts typically (1) state that the record company owns all rights, including the sound recording copyrights (and all the potential ways these can make money), in works that are created by the artist under the recording contract, and (2) provide the record company with the right to a certain number of albums and an option for others. Our example contract stated:

> Artist shall deliver new Masters and completed Artwork for
> additional option albums to the specifications described below

at the request of Recording Company, up to and including five additional Option Masters. . . .

Said Option Masters shall be recorded according to the budget provided by Recording Company and described below and said recordings shall remain the property of Recording Company in perpetuity.

At this point, the contract goes from bad to worse in two significant ways. First, a five-album option is a lot. The record company is going to exercise the option only if it is a good deal for the company. If it is unhappy with the deal, it will not exercise the option. So, the fewer option albums you can give the record company the better. If the record company insists upon extensive options, at a minimum, you should negotiate for increased royalties for the later albums. Second, transferring rights to the record company in perpetuity means that the record company can continue to sell the option albums after termination of the agreement, regardless of the basis for its termination. You should consider having a sunset provision on these rights, which sets forth when these rights end.

If a record company has done little to exploit your recordings for a substantial period of time, why should you not be able to monetize those recordings on your own? The original record company should not be able to ride the coattails of someone who later puts in the time and effort to popularize the work. Consider, for example, after the term has expired, you re-record the songs and spend substantial sums marketing and promoting the new album. It is unfair for the original record company to profit off of those efforts.

Delivery

As mentioned above, our example contract required delivery of masters per the "specifications described below." This portion of our example contract required:

(1) no less than ten (10) previously unreleased songs and forty-five (45) minutes of new previously unrecorded music performed by the Artist, (2) a commercially and technically satisfactory Master approved by the Recording Company, (3) sideman clearances, and (4) all mechanical licenses for each musical composition at the rate of 75% of the statutory rate.

Here again, our example contract favors the record company in at least two ways. First, it provides the company substantial control over whether the new master is acceptable. A more balanced provision might be one that requires that the new master be of the same style and quality of the artist's prior work. Second, this provision requires that the royalty paid to the author of the compositions be 75% of the statutory rate. So, in the first instance, this reduces the artist's royalty on the artist's compositions included in the album. As explained above, for an album with 10 compositions, that could be 91 cents per album. Also, consider that if any of the compositions on the album were written by someone else, the artist would need to negotiate a license with the owner(s) of those compositions (or usually with the Harry Fox Agency) that would allow the record company to compensate them, and they may not accept 75% of the statutory rate. This will likely require the artist to come up with money out of his own pocket to obtain those rights.

Artwork

Our example contract also required the artist to deliver artwork for each of the option albums. In other words, the artist needs to pay for the artwork. Again, this is money out of the artist's pocket. Sometimes a record company will advance the costs for the artwork and the expense associated with the artwork is taken out of the artist's share of royalties. Whether you enter into a recording contract or not, it is often the case that artists will engage a friend or two to help them with album art or photographs. It is important to make sure that you properly acquire the rights to those works. This is discussed in more detail in chapter 9.

Budgets

As also mentioned above, our example contract required: "Said Option Masters shall be recorded according to the budget provided by Recording Company and described below."

The budget provision of our example contract provides:

> Budgets for the recording of additional Option Albums shall be determined by multiplying the total number of sales of the immediately preceding album release by one dollar, less any unrecouped balance in Artist's royalty account. . . . Regardless of Artist's sales totals, all recording budgets shall provide a minimum of $1,000 to Artist up to a maximum of $20,000, 50% to be paid on commencement of recording and 50% upon delivery.

So, what is wrong with this provision? Well, what if the artist never earns enough to recoup his advances? The record company can exercise the option with a measly $1,000 payment to the artist. And because the sales of the previous albums are largely in the control of the record company, the artist in our example contract could be bound to this record company for years, all in exchange for the initial advance (which is discussed below) and $1,000 per album.

As an artist, you should insist that the record company set a realistic budget for any option albums. The record company should have to make a renewed investment before exercising its options.

Advances

Most recording contracts provide the artists with an advance that is recouped against royalty payments. In other words, if the advance is $10,000, an artist will not receive any royalties until the advance has been recouped. Our example contract provided for a $2,000 advance conditioned upon the delivery of the masters for the prior albums. A $2,000 advance is on the low end of the low range for advances. You have to question how much a record company really believes in you and your music when they are unwilling to pay a reasonable advance.

The amount of an advance varies greatly depending upon the amount of success an artist has achieved at the time of entering into the agreement. You should research what common advances are for artists that have achieved your level of success before entering into a record deal.

Recoupment

Every recording contract that we have reviewed has stated that monies paid to the artist as advances, and monies paid to record, produce, market, and promote the recordings, shall be treated as advances, and that all advances are to be recouped out of the artist's share of royalties. In other words, other than any advance received, an artist is not going to receive any royalties until the record company has been reimbursed for all of the expenses it has laid out in connection with the creation, marketing, promotion, etc. of the album. Our example contract had such a provision (in fact, for good measure, the provision was set out in two separate places in the contract).

Royalties

Almost all recording contracts also have a provision setting out the royalties that the artist will earn on the sale of records. Our example contract provided:

> Artist royalties will be calculated bi-annually and calculated as 12% of the retail list price on 90% of all product sold and for which Recording Company received payment from their distributors or licensees, with 25% being held for returns. The return reserve will be liquidated in equal installments during each of the bi-annual accounting periods in the third year following initial release.

As you can probably guess by now, the record company in our example contract got the better of the deal in several ways. First, a 12 percent royalty is low. Royalties are typically between 13 percent and 20 percent. Second, sales on 90 percent of albums *sold and paid for* is inappropriate. While historically paying royalties on 90 percent of albums shipped was fairly common (justified because of breakage, etc.), it is an antiquated provision that is rarely used today, and it has absolutely no place in a contract that pays royalties based upon records that have been sold *and paid for*. For what it is worth, the reserve holdback is common (because distributors have a guaranteed right to return unsold records), especially for new artists.

Publishing Rights

Although most major record companies will not do so, some smaller record companies will push for rights in your compositions (as opposed to the sound recordings) embodied in the recordings contained on the album created under the contract, as well as the monetization rights that come with them. Do not give up rights in your compositions. ***Do not do it!*** The record company is unlikely to do anything to assist you in the creation or enhancement of these compositions or enhance their exploitation. Think about it like this: If you were recording someone else's composition (which you have a statutory right to do after the composition is first published), your record company would not get any right to those compositions. Why should it be any different because you created the composition? Unfortunately, our example contract provided just that:

> Artist hereby irrevocably and absolutely assigns, conveys, and sets over to Recording Company an undivided interest in the copyright (and all renewals and extensions thereof) in perpetuity and all other rights in and to each original Composition contained on each Album Master released under this Agreement, provided that the [previously created compositions] shall revert to Artist upon recoupment of all the above stated recording and marketing Advances.

Not only does this provision purport to require the artist to assign all of his composition rights to the record company, the record company might argue that it even requires the artist to have secured the rights to all of the compositions (even those written by others, or co-authored with another artist). To the extent you feel you must give a record company a portion of your publishing rights, try to maintain control of those publishing rights and share a percentage with the record company, and/or try to limit the revenue sources that you share with the record company, i.e. ASCAP/BMI/SESAC receipts.

Other Provisions

As mentioned above, there are a host of other provisions that are commonly contained in a recording contract. It is beyond the scope of this book to analyze them all. When you get to the point of negotiating the finer points of a recording contract, this would be a good time—if not earlier—to bring in an attorney knowledgeable and experienced with such contracts.

Chapter 8

The Helping Hands?

You and your band have your band agreement in place, and you have written songs and are playing local gigs. You may have even recorded some of your sessions at a local recording studio. But, you realize you need help if you really want to start getting exposure and making real money. As you probably already know, there are many types of service that help out bands just like yours: booking agents, record producers, sound engineers, session players, and managers to name a few. After identifying, interviewing and selecting who you want to help your band, you should enter into a contract with them so that there are no surprises down the road. And, unfortunately, if you do not have a written agreement, you may be surprised to find out that the booking agent you hired believes that she is entitled to an equal share in all the profit you generated (including from album and merchandising sales) at a concert she helped you land, or, years later, that the record producer you hired believes he is a co-owner of all the songs you recorded with him. This chapter will go over the key provisions that you should include in your agreements with these helping hands.

Booking Agents

Booking agents can help you land your own shows, or bring you in as the opening act for other bands, which as you have likely discovered requires a great deal of effort. The booking agent agreement is a pretty straight-forward agreement. The key provisions include exclusivity or non-exclusivity, the term or length of the agreement, the booking agent's compensation, and power of attorney. Before entering into any contract with a booking agent, you must be aware of the dormant booking agent. Many booking agents seem personable, energetic, enthusiastic and well connected before they sign a band. But, after signing a long-term contract with the band, they do very little to promote the band and get them into venues. Understandably, these bands get frustrated with the fact that they are not getting any performances, and start looking for and landing gigs on their own. When they secure a performance, guess who has their hand out insisting on their percentage? Of course, not all booking agents are dormant, but you must protect yourself just in case.

"Exclusivity or non-exclusivity" refers to whether your band is agreeing that only one booking agent will be actively trying to get shows for your band. An exclusive booking agent agreement is an agreement where there is only one booking agent; whereas, a non-exclusive agreement is one where there is more than one booking agent. Most booking agent agreements are exclusive, as this avoids scheduling conflicts and disputes that may otherwise arise as to which booking agent was responsible for landing the show. However, especially if this is a new relationship, placing all your hopes in this agent's hands is probably not very comforting. You should discuss with your potential booking agents whether your band remains free to identify opportunities to perform, and, if it finds a show, what the booking agent's payment will be in that situation. You may also want to discuss elimination of exclusivity if the booking agent does not meet certain thresholds, such as $10,000 in appearance fees in every six month period. These agreements should be set out in your contract with the booking agent.

The term of the booking agent agreement will establish how long you will be working with the booking agent. The term is usually one year. A related issue is the so-called "sunset provision." Consider the situation where a booking agent has been working to get you in as the opening act for a hot band during the term of the agreement. The agreement terminates and the drummer from this hot band contacts your lead singer and asks if you would open for them. Your band is promised a nice appearance fee, so you accept. After the show, the booking agent insists she is entitled to a percentage of your appearance fee. Should the booking agent get a percentage? The answer to this question is usually spelled out in the sunset provision, which sets out when certain rights end. Obviously, the shorter this sunset provision is the better for your band, and you may want to require your booking agent to provide you with a list of deals she had been working on when your agreement terminates, and written documentation demonstrating legitimate efforts.

A standard booking agent agreement usually includes compensation anywhere between 10-20%, which of course is negotiable. Importantly, however, you must be careful how compensation is defined in the agreement. Does it include just the appearance fee, or does it include record and merchandise sales? These are all negotiable items.

Finally, a booking agent must be provided with a limited power of attorney, which allows the booking agent to act on the group's behalf when booking gigs and appearances. Note, however, you should be very careful when drafting the power of attorney clause as to not give the booking agent too much power. The power of attorney should only permit the booking agent to commit your band to appear at the show being booked and conduct itself as required by the venue to secure the performance.

Modern Trends

Recently, there has been a surge of third party booking websites. These websites cut out the middleman when negotiating with venues. They allow the venue or band to search online and connect directly with the other party, saving time and money. These websites are typically non-exclusive, charge a flat rate fee for their service, and operate under a form service agreement on their webpage. These agreements are almost always non-negotiable. If one of these websites spark your interest, make sure to have an attorney read the online service agreement so your group knows exactly what they are signing.

Producers

While your first recordings were great, your band realizes that it could benefit from an experienced producer who can provide guidance on song selection, add a keen ear and musical suggestions, and bring in session musicians, vocalists and a sound engineer. There are key provisions of the contract that your band should pay attention to when entering into an agreement with the producer. These include the roles and expectations of the producer, ownership of the copyrights, and producer compensation.

Regarding copyright ownership, if a producer (or any of the musicians, vocalists or sound engineers hired by the producer to assist in the process) makes creative contributions to your musical compositions, the producer would be considered a co-author and co-owner of those sound recordings under copyright law. Similarly, if the producer or her employees makes creative contributions to your sound recordings, the producer would be a co-author and co-owner of the sound recordings as well.

As explained earlier, under copyright law, when two or more authors work together and intend their contributions to be merged into inseparable and interdependent parts of a unitary whole, those authors are consider joint authors. One can easily envision how this might apply in a situation when a producer is retained to assist in the creation of a sound recording. Therefore, but for an appropriate written agreement being in place, the producer you hire to help you perfect your sound recording may end up as an equal owner of the underlying compositions and recordings. Most artist and producers do not intend that result. But, nevertheless, early in their careers, many bands ignore the need for a contract for this situation. As explained in Chapter 3, there are two primary methods to ensure that rights in the copyrights remain with the band: an assignment and/or a work-made-for-hire agreement. Provisions such as those found in Appendix C and D setting forth that the producer's contributions are either assigned or works-made-for-hire should be contained in the agreement. A typical provision may looking something like this:

Copyrights:

Any contribution to any of the songs listed in this Agreement, and their recordings, will be considered a work-made-for-hire for Recording Artist, if any such contribution is deemed not to be a work-made-for-hire, all rights, title, and interest in the contribution which is attributable to the Producer, or any of the session musicians, vocalists, and sound engineers provided by Producer in connection with the performance of this agreement will be deemed transferred to Recording Artist by this Agreement. This Agreement may be filed with the Register of Copyright as an official transfer of copyright. All compositions and recordings thereof listed under this Agreement shall be the sole property of Recording Artist, free from any claims whatsoever by Producer or any other person; and Recording Artist shall have the exclusive right to claim ownership of and register the copyright to those compositions and sound recordings in his name and to secure any and all renewals and extensions of such copyright throughout the world.

Producers are typically paid an advance plus a percentage of revenue generated from the sound recordings. A producer compensation provision may look something like this:

Compensations:

a) Conditioned upon Producer's full and faithful performance of all the terms and provisions hereof, Artist shall pay Producer, as an advance recoupable by Artist from any and all royalties payable by Artist to Producer hereunder, the sum of $ _____ DOLLARS, half payable upon commencement of recording, and the balance upon the delivery to Artist of the Masters.

b) Producer shall be paid in respect to the sale of such phonorecords a royalty rate of three percent (3%) of the suggested retail price of each phonorecord sold and paid for in the United States. Payments of royalties from foreign sources shall be ONE HALF of the United States royalty rate. All fees paid to Producer hereunder shall constitute recoupable advances which shall be recouped prior to further payment of royalties.

There are many other provisions to be wary of when negotiating an agreement with a producer, so it is advised you hire an attorney to help your group through the negotiation process.

Session Players and Sound Engineers

As mentioned above, producers may bring in sound engineers and sessions players during the production of your band's recordings. If they are employees of the Producer, then their contributions are owned by the producer as works-made-for-hire, and the contractual provisions set forth above will make sure that your band will retain the copyright in those contributions. If the sound engineers and session players are not employees of the producers, or, if your band chooses to forgo a producer and retain session players and/ or sound engineers directly, it is very important to have a contract with these sound engineers and sessions players as well. Again, the crucial provision in a sound engineer or session player contract revolves around whether the contract makes the contributions of the engineer or player a work-made-for-hire.

360° Deals:

When looking at a recording contract, be wary of the modern trend of "360° Deals." These are all encompassing deals offered by record labels. The record label agrees to cover all of the bands services such as concert booking, merchandise sales, and endorsement deals in addition to a traditional record label contract. While this may sound like a great "one-stop shop" mentality for bands, the record label will also want a much larger percentage. These deals tend to benefit the record label more than the band because it entitles the label to a percentage of more wide-ranging services than a traditional recording contract while at the same time decreasing the risk of signing bands. It decreases the risk because the record label controls all aspects of the band and can focus on the idea of "band branding." Despite these contracts favoring the record label, they are still something to think about when starting a band because it eliminates a lot of extra work the band may have to do, i.e. searching for separate booking agents and publicists.

Chapter 9

How Do We Get Permission to Use
Artwork and Photos?

As mentioned earlier, as an artist you are likely to produce your first album or two on your own. In doing so, you will likely want to create interesting cover art. You may also want to have photographs of the band included as cover art and to use as promotional material. And, of course, you are going to want cool merchandise to sell at your gigs, which will inevitably include designs and characters created by others.

It is important that your band obtain the rights to this artwork before you start using and distributing it. Just like your compositions and recordings are copyrightable material, drawings, paintings, and photographs are also copyrightable. As such, even if you buy an individual copy of this art, you are not authorized to copy and distribute it or to use it on items such as T-shirts.

If you ask the creator of the artwork for the rights to the work at the time you are getting started and before the work is created, it is usually easy to get the artist to agree to these uses of the work. On the other hand, if you wait until the work has been wrongfully distributed and obtained recognition, imagine how difficult the negotiation might be. But what should that agreement look like? Should it be a license from the artist allowing your band to use the work in connection with your music business? Or should it be an assignment to the band?

Without an assignment of the work to the band, you will not be able to prevent others from using the artwork. This would be the responsibility of the artist to control other uses of her work. Many times, both the creator of the artwork and the band using the artwork would prefer that the creator not be involved. In that situation, an assignment is the preferred approach. A few points to keep in mind in connection with such an agreement:

(1) It must be in writing;

(2) It should be short and simple;

(3) It should provide the artist with compensation (even if only a small amount, such as a $1);

(4) It should attach the artwork being assigned;

(5) It should require the artist to assist in enforcing rights related to the art; and

(6) It should be notarized.

An example assignment agreement is attached as Appendix E at the end of this book.

Chapter 10

Partnership, Corporation, or
Limited Liability Company?

As discussed in Chapter 1, if you are committed to and serious about coming together as a working band, you should enter into an band agreement as soon as possible. We opened the book with that discussion because of how important such an agreement is in operating efficiently and effectively. An additional consideration, which would be included in the agreement but which is a discussion unto itself, is the actual structure of your band's operations. We address three common structures here: partnerships, corporations, and limited liability companies.

Your choice of business entity for your band is largely dependent on weighing the potential risks of personal liability for the actions of the band and other band members against the added costs of filing as an LLC or the ongoing requirements of filing as an "S" corporation. At the very least, you should begin to consider your options. And again, regardless of which structure you choose, your band should have an internal band agreement that controls ownership of the works being created by the band and sets out clearly the expectations of the band members while the band is active, and the rights of the individual band members when the band breaks up.

Partnership

The chief advantage of a partnership is that it is simple. There are minimal startup requirements, there is flexibility in structuring the band's operations, and there are very few (if any) requirements that you file documents with the state. A "general" partnership is the simplest and least expensive form of partnership. There are no forms that must be filed with the state to create or maintain a general partnership. Therefore, no filing fees are associated with establishing your band as a general partnership.

The main disadvantage of choosing a partnership as your business structure is that each band member can be held *personally* responsible for the acts and debts of the band as an entity, and the acts of your bandmates on behalf of the band. For instance, if someone attending one of your concerts was injured by a speaker that fell off the stage, you and the rest of the band might be held personally liable. This means your *personal assets*—the money in your personal bank account, your car, or even your prized Les Paul—may be at risk to satisfy the debts that the band cannot afford to pay.

Let's say down the road your band gets popular. One of your bandmates gets a gig for your band, signs a contract with the promoter agreeing to play the gig, accepts a deposit of $10,000, does not tell anyone else about it, and then skips town. The rest of you do not show up for the gig (because you do not even know about it!) and break the contract. That promoter wants his money back, and suddenly, you and the remaining band members have become liable for the $10,000. And because there is what is referred to as joint and several liability for partnerships, any band member could be made to pay the *entire* amount of damages in a lawsuit, rather than splitting it evenly between all the members. The band member who has to pay, of course, could try to get the other band members to pay their share, but that may not be possible.

These are just two examples of the different types of liabilities that could arise under a general partnership. In addition to the problem of personal liability, there are many other reasons why a general partnership might not be the best option for your band. Unless your band agreement states otherwise, most states' default partnership rules would dictate, among other things, that all members of the band would share in the band's profits equally and have equal rights in the management and conduct of the band, with ordinary matters decided by majority vote. However, the default rules do not address many issues that bands face, such as day-to-day band operations, potentially unequal distribution of profits, and, importantly, what happens when a band member leaves the group. If you do not have a band agreement or if your band agreement does not specifically address an issue, as a general partnership, the state's default partnership rules will likely apply even if those rules are not how the band would have wanted it at the outset.

"S" Corporation

The government allows small businesses to be formed as "S" corporations. This type of entity provides shareholders (the band members) with limited liability protection (like an LLC, discussed below), and your profits are only taxed once (also like an LLC). Additionally, "S" corporations may have lower filing and annual costs than LLCs (in Illinois, for example, there is a $150 filing fee and $75 in annual costs for "S" corporations).

The drawbacks to filing as an "S" corporation are the rigid management structure rules and the onerous ongoing requirements. For example, "S" corporations permit a limited number of shareholders and do not allow voting and non-voting members. While these might seem complicated and irrelevant to you and your band's needs right now, it is important to realize that these limits can restrict the way you may want to operate in the future. In addition to the rigid management structure, there are also many ongoing requirements—for example, you must have regular band meetings and keep written minutes detailing what was discussed at the meetings. You should consider the fact that complying with the increased operating requirements comes at a cost, both in money and time.

Limited Liability Company ("LLC")

An LLC provides many of the advantages of a partnership (such as management flexibility), while also offering liability protection for its members. As a member of an LLC, your liability for the acts and debts of the band and its members acting on its behalf would be limited to the amount you invested into the band. Your personal assets (*e.g.*, your home, car, bank account) would not be put at risk. Rather, only the band itself can be held liable for debts—not the individual band members. Even if your band doesn't have any money in the bank, your personal bank account and assets would remain safe. Further, as the owner of an LLC, you and your bandmates would have the freedom to organize and run the band almost any way you want. LLC laws are flexible in terms of ownership, decision making, and revenue distribution.

The downside of filing as an LLC is the added cost of its formation and the annual fees a state collects. States vary on the amount required to file and annual fees; as one example, in Illinois, it costs $500 to file and $250 in annual fees. Some states have additional requirements for forming LLCs. In Illinois, once an LLC is formed, bands are required to file an annual report. If the annual report is not filed within 60 days after the due date, the company will be placed in a "penalty status" and a late-filing penalty may be imposed. If the annual report is still not filed within 120 days, the entity will be administratively dissolved.

So, while there are definite advantages to becoming an LLC, there are also costs and requirements with which your band must comply. If your band does not make enough money to warrant such an expense, it might be best to hold off until the time is right. However, if your band is investing a lot of money in equipment, merchandise, and travel, you may want to consider formally creating an LLC or S corporation so that your assets can be protected. For specific details on how to form as a business entity, check with the Illinois Secretary of State's office at cyberdriveillinois.com.

Chapter 11

How Do We Break Up?

As the saying goes, all good things must come to an end. So if the time has come for your band to part ways—whether through creative differences, other family or work obligations, or your band devolving into a chaotic, contentious mess filled with scandal and infighting—here are 10 issues to keep in mind when splitting up.

1. Follow Your Band Agreement

If you have followed the advice in this book, your band has entered into a band agreement. This agreement should set forth the rights and obligations of the band members upon termination of the agreement, and it should provide a blueprint for how you have agreed to break up. As such, you should first consult your band agreement when breaking up. Doing so could streamline the process, as long as you and your bandmates agree to follow what you had initially agreed to. Of course, if there is disagreement in the band about a possible breach of the band agreement, then the agreement may not serve its intended purpose.

2. Pay Your Bills

As discussed in the previous chapter, if your band is a partnership, then each member of the band can be personally liable for the debts of the band. So if you have outstanding bills for rehearsal space, time in the recording studio, merchandise, or payments on your touring van, you should work together to resolve these debts. Otherwise, creditors could end up chasing individual band members for debts they are unable to pay, which would be unfair to make an individual member pay.

3. Communicate With Your Record Label

If you have entered into a recording contract, such as the one discussed in Chapter 7, a clause may exist in the contract regarding the band's obligations to the label if it breaks up as a group. You should consult your record deal and see what obligations may exist. You should also make sure to let your record label know of the breakup. And if you think that you may have problems with the label, you should consider consulting with an attorney and perhaps have the attorney initiate these conversations and negotiate your deal with the record label.

4. Who Owns Your Masters?

If you have entered into a recording contract, the record company may very well own your master recordings. But if you have recorded and released your own music, the band probably controls the masters. Of course, your band agreement should have addressed ownership of your master recordings, and if this was not addressed in your band agreement, it should have been addressed before or after your recording sessions. Dealing with ownership issues when breaking up is not the ideal situation—especially in a contentious split—but if this has not been addressed before this point, it is vital to resolve these issues immediately.

5. Who Owns Your Compositions?

Again, as discussed earlier in this book, this issue should be taken care of well before breaking up, either in the band agreement or in a letter of agreement for particular compositions or groups of compositions. However, if there is any question of composition ownership upon breaking up—for example, ownership of partially written compositions—this should be addressed. Perhaps these compositions will have little to no value down the road. However, as discussed in previous chapters, compositions can create significant revenue streams well into the future. So if one of your band's compositions becomes a hit—either your version or a cover version—knowing who should receive public performance and mechanical royalties is essential, as is knowing who has the ability to negotiate synchronization or print licenses for these compositions.

6. The Band Name

Again, this is an issue that should be addressed in the band agreement. But if there is a question on who owns and who can use the band's name (so as to avoid what happened with Black Sabbath), this should be resolved. Decide if the band name should be buried, or if a particular band member can continue using it. Also, the trademark registration should be assigned if there is a new owner of the name.

7. Receiving and Distributing Royalties

Just because the band breaks up does not mean that your royalty streams will suddenly dry up. Again, this may sound like a broken record, but control of these compositions and sound recordings should be handled in a band agreement. But if this is an open issue, you must decide who will receive and distribute to the other band members royalties from places such as the PRO handling your public performance royalties (ASCAP, BMI, SESAC), your publisher, Harry Fox, SoundExchange, etc. And if you do not think that a particular member of your band can handle this work, you should hire someone to manage these royalties as they come in. In addition, you should notify these companies if royalties have to be sent to a different person.

8. Control of Your Web Site, Facebook Account, Twitter Account, and Mailing Lists

You have worked hard to create a huge e-mail list, build your Facebook friends, get followers on Twitter or Tumblr, and build a robust, content-rich website. These have significant value, and should not be taken for granted. Of course, you should update your website and other digital media to let your fans know of the end of the group. And you should also come to an agreement about what you are going to do with these valuable lists of names and followers. For example, does everyone in the band have access to these? If it was a bad split, what if one band member uses the mailing list to disparage the other members? In short, make sure to have a plan about who will control your contacts and digital communications.

9.   Leftover CDs and Other Merchandise, and Outstanding Gigs

Maybe you purchased boxes of CDs from your record label or have self-recorded an album, and you have lots of leftover CDs. Maybe you have boxes of T-shirts and posters. Besides having sentimental value, these goods can have actual value. Make sure you divvy these up accordingly. Likewise, you may have some gigs scheduled down the road. You have to notify the promoter that you will not be making the gig. Hopefully, there is a clause in the contract that allows you to back out of the gig without liability in the event the band breaks up. Make sure to do this for all of your shows.

10. Do a Final Accounting

After you have dealt with all of your bills and put your band in order to break up, you should do a final accounting. If you have a bank account, after you have paid your bills, you can close it. If you owe an accountant or attorney their fees, don't forget to pay these, or to leave some money on the side to cover these costs to wrap up the band. And when you think you have resolved your debts and other obligations, using the procedures set forth in your band agreement, you should close your books and move on to your next musical adventure.

Losing The Bassist—A Partial Breakup

What if your band does not break up, but only a member or two has to leave the group? The following agreement could be used as a model if one of your bandmates splits.

PARTNERSHIP RESIGNATION AND COMPENSATION AGREEMENT

WHEREAS [Partners] (individually, "Partners") entered into a Band Agreement related to their business ("Band Agreement"), operating under the name [Band Name] (the "Band");

WHEREAS the Band Agreement provides that upon the resignation of a partner, the resigning partner shall be entitled to the same compensation of a disassociated partner, less the damage caused the Partnership by his departure;

WHEREAS the Band Agreement generally provides that a disassociated partner shall be entitled to receive a proportionate share of the net worth of the partnership as determined by an independent accountant; and a pro rata share of received royalties earned from the exploitation of any phonorecord recorded under the Band Agreement that embodies the disassociating partner's performance, less a pro rata share of expenses ("Future Royalties");

WHEREAS each of the Partners entered into a Lyric and Music Ownership Agreement generally granting the Partnership all rights to any Contributions (as defined therein) of the Partner incorporated in any sound recording of the Band, and therefore all rights in the composition for any song performed by the Band are considered assets of the Band;

WHEREAS [Departing Member] ("[First Name of Departing Member]") has retired from the Band;

WHEREAS each of the Partners, including [First Name of Departing Member], agree that it would be cost prohibitive to retain an independent accountant to determine [First Name of Departing Member]' Compensation and desire to eliminate the requirement of accounting to [First Name of Departing Member] for Future Royalties; and

THEREFORE, it is agreed as follows:

[First Name of Departing Member] relinquishes any and all claims to [First Name of Departing Member]' Compensation and Future Royalties, and any and all ownership interest in the Partnership and its assets, present or future.

Agreed to this ____ [DATE], by:

Website Resources

Lawyers for the Creative Arts... www.law-arts.org

ASCAP ....www.ascap.com

Audiosocket... www.audiosocket.com

BMI.. www.bmi.com

CD Baby .... www.cdbaby.com

Harry Fox Agency ....www.harryfox.com

Illinois Secretary of State .... www.cyberdriveillinois.com

INgrooves .... www.ingrooves.com

Music Dealers..www.musicdealers.com

Nimbit... www.nimbit.com

Redeye .... www.redeyeusa.com

ReverbNation.. www.reverbnation.com

SESAC..www.sesac.com

SoundExchange ....www.soundexchange.com

The Orchard..www.iodalliance.com

TuneCore .... www.tunecore.com

U.S. Copyright Office.. www.copyright.gov

U.S. Patent and Trademark Office ....www.uspto.gov

Appendix A

BAND AGREEMENT

This Agreement is made and entered into as of [INSERT DATE] by and between Partner A, Partner B, Partner C, Partner D, and Partner E (hereinafter individually referred to as "Partner" and collectively as "Partners," "Band," or "Group"):

WHEREAS, the Partners have been and are conducting business as a partnership under the name of BAND, pursuant to a previous implied agreement, under which each of the Partners has been sharing in the profits and losses; and

WHEREAS, the Partners desire to continue conducting their business as a partnership and to commit their agreement to writing;

AND, in consideration of the mutual covenants hereinafter contained, it is hereby agreed as follows:

1. <u>FORMATION</u>:

The Partners hereby constitute themselves as a General Partnership (the "Partnership") under laws of the State of [_____].

2. <u>NAME OF PARTNERSHIP</u>:

The Partnership shall operate and conduct business under the name of Band.

3. <u>TERM</u>:

The Partnership shall commence on [DATE] and shall continue thereafter until dissolved in any manner provided herein.

4. <u>PLACE OF BUSINESS</u>:

The principal office and place of business of the Partnership shall be located at [ADDRESS OF BAND OFFICE] or such other place as the Partners may from time to time designate.

5. <u>PURPOSE</u>:

The purpose of the Partnership is for the Partners to engage in the entertainment, recording, and publishing industries (the "entertainment field") as the musical group BAND including, without limitation, recording commercial phonorecords, performing personal appearances, exploiting and merchandising the names (both legal and professional), likeness, sobriquet and biographical materials ("Merchandising Rights") of each Partner, either individually or collectively as members of the Group, and the Group Name. However, the Partners are free to render their services in the entertainment field to other entities, or individually, so long as it does not interfere with their obligations to the partnership described herein.

6. COMPOSITIONS

Compositions written by the Partners are owned by the Partners that collaborated in the creation of the composition. Prior to performing or publishing any sound recordings embodying these compositions, the Partners will complete a Composition Copyright Split Agreement establishing those Partners that collaborated in the creation of the composition.

7. DUTIES:

(a) General Duties:

Each partner agrees to participate in at least six of the nine hours per week designated by the Partnership for practice; appear and perform at all performances, unless excused by unanimous approval of the Partners or provided said unexcused absences do not exceed two in any given six month time frame; and make a good faith effort to complete the respective designated duties described below; and to fully perform any and all activities unanimously agreed upon by the partners.

(b) Specific Duties:

Each of the Partners is herby assigned the following duties:

(i) Partner A- public relations

(ii) Partners B and C - promotion

(iii) Partner D - accounting

(iv) Partner E - negotiating and entering into contracts

8. CONTRIBUTIONS:

(a) Initial Contributions:

As a contribution to the Partnership, each Partner is contributing his services in the entertainment field including, without limitations, service as a recording artist with respect to phonorecords which may be recorded and exploited by the Partnership hereunder, services as a musical performer, and his rights to Merchandising Rights.

(b) Instruments, Equipment, Etc.:

All of the instruments, musical, sound, and video equipment owned by each Partner and used in connection with the activities of the Partnership shall continue to belong to such Partner according to such Partner's present ownership therein, but during the term of the Partnership, during which such Partner shall remain a Partner, the Partnership shall be entitled to the full use thereof, free of expense, except for insurance and repairs. And all partners shall be directly responsible for obtaining necessary additional, replacement, or substitute equipment as subsequently determined by the Partner or a 2/3 majority of the Partnership. However, all other equipment hereafter acquired in connection with the Partnership activities shall be paid for from the Partnership monies and shall be deemed additional capital of the Partnership.

(c) Additional Capital:

Whenever it is determined by a 2/3 majority of the Partners that the capital of the Partnership is likely to become insufficient for the conduct of the Partnership business, the Partners shall make additional capital contributions in the proportions in which such Partners are then entitled to share in the profits of the Partnership.

(d) Failure to Make Capital Contributions:

If any Partner fails to make any contribution to the Partnership's capital at the time and in the amount required by this Agreement, any other Partner may, at its sole discretion, loan money to said defaulting Partner on such terms as may be agreed upon by the parties or, in the alternative, may withdraw its own capital contribution and instead lend money to the Partnership pursuant to Clause 9 below.

(e) Withdrawals of Capital:

No Partner may withdraw capital from the Partnership without the unanimous agreement of the Partners.

9. LOANS TO PARTNERSHIP:

Any loans to the Partnership (whether from the Partners or from unrelated third parties) shall be payable by the Partnership on such terms as the parties shall mutually agree, may bear reasonable interest and shall constitute an obligation of the Partnership which shall be prior to the return of capital or any distribution provided herein.

10. DIVISION OF PROFITS AND LOSSES:

The Partnership's profits and losses shall be shared equally by the Partners.

11. DISTRIBUTION OF PROFITS:

(a) Net profits shall be distributed in cash to the Partners according to the terms described herein or as expressly authorized by the unanimous consent of the Partners. The aggregate amounts distributed to the Partners from the Partnership's profits shall not, however, exceed the amount of cash available for distribution, taking into account the Partnership's reasonable working capital.

(b) Within two (2) days after the Partnership is paid for a performance, the income shall be distributed in the following manner. All expenses related to the performance shall be paid. From the remainder, after payment of expenses: ten percent (10%) shall be deposited in the Partnership bank account; each Partner shall receive five percent (5%); and the rest shall be divided equally amount the performing Partners. If, however, a non-performing Partner missed the performance without the consent of the remaining Partners, that Partner shall lose the rights to all profits related to that performance, including but not limited to his share of the profits attributed to sales of merchandise sold at the performance.

(c) Within ten (10) working days after the end of each month, there shall be distributed in cash to the Partners in proportion to their respective shares in the Partnership's profits, the Partnership's net profits from all other Partnership activities less ten percent (10%) which shall be deposited in the Partnership's bank account.

(d) For the purpose of this agreement, "net profits" as used herein shall mean all income, commissions, royalties, bonuses, payments (other than repayment of loans), dividends, stock bonuses, interests, or monies of any kind or nature paid to the Partnership or to any Partner (except as provided in Clauses 8 and 9 above) as a result of the Partnership's or any Partner's activities in the entertainment field after deducting the sum total of all reasonable salaries, management and agency fees, rent, promotional costs, travel costs, office expenditures, telephone costs, accounting and legal fees, entertainment costs, and any and all legitimate Partnership expenses incurred by the Partnership while conducting Partnership business.

(e) The Partners shall be entitled to draw from time to time against the net profits of the Partnership so credited to their respective accounts in such amounts which may be agreed upon by the unanimous consent of the Partners. Any profits distributed in accordance with the foregoing shall be less any sum which any Partner may have previously drawn on account thereof, and if it is determined that any Partner shall have drawn out more than his share of the profits, such Partner shall immediately repay the excess to the Partnership.

(f) Except as provided in paragraph 11(b), no Partner shall receive a salary, bonus, or goods or other assets of that Partnership in excess of that received by any other Partner, except upon the unanimous vote of all the Partners.

12. MANAGEMENT:

Each Partner shall have one vote on all matters to be decided by the Partnership and shall have the right to participate equally in the control, management, and direction of the business of the Partnership. A two-thirds (2/3) affirmative vote of the Partners shall be required to adopt any Partnership decision, except that a unanimous vote of the Partners shall be required in the following matters:

1. Making any amendment to this Agreement, except an amendment by operation of law, in the event of a death of a Partner. Said Partner's right to vote on any Partnership matter shall terminate with his death.

2. Making any expenditure on behalf of the Partnership in excess of $1,000.

3. Borrowing money in the Partnership's name or making, executing, delivering, or guaranteeing any commercial paper, compromise, or release of debts owing to the Partnership.

4. Disposing of the good will of the Partnership.

5. Pledging or transferring in any matter any interest in the Partnership except to another Partner.

The following two decisions are to be made upon the unanimous approval of all partners with the exception of the Partner or proposed Partner that will be directly affected by the decision, who shall not vote:

6. Determining that a Partner is under permanent disability, that a Partner shall be expelled from the Partnership or that a Partner shall be added to the Partnership as described more fully herein; and

7. Consenting that a Partner may miss a performance without suffering a "penalty" as defined herein, such consent not to be unreasonably withheld.

13. MEETINGS OF PARTNERS:

Partnership meetings will be held monthly. Further, upon reasonable notice, a majority of the Partners may, from time to time, elect to call a meeting of the Partners at any reasonable time at the Partnership's principal place of business. In such event, any and all expenses incurred by the Partners in attending such meeting shall be borne solely by each said Partner unless a majority of the Partners agree otherwise.

14. NEW PARTNERS:

A new Partner may be admitted to the Partnership but only with the unanimous written consent of the Partners. A new Partner shall be admitted only if he executes an agreement with the Partnership under the terms of which such Partner agrees to be bound by all of the provisions hereof, as amended, as if a signatory hereto. Unless expressly agreed upon by the unanimous vote of the Partners, such new Partner shall have no interest whatsoever in the Group Name apart from the limited right to be known as a member of the Group. Such new Partner's capital contribution, if any, and share of the Partnership's net profits and losses shall be agreed upon in the written consent of all of the Partners approving the admission of the new Partner.

15. PARTNER'S DEATH OR DISABILITY:

(a) A Partner may become disassociated from the Partnership by reason of his death or disability. For the purposes hereof, the term "disability" shall include, without limitation, the inability of a Partner to render the services described herein for a continuous period of six (6) months. A Partner (or, in the event of disassociation by death, his executor or personal representative) who is disassociated shall be entitled to receive an amount equal to his proportionate share of the net worth of the Partnership as of the date of his disassociation, but he shall not be entitled to any of the earnings of the Partnership received thereafter, nor shall he have any interest in the Group name except as provided herein, nor shall he be subject to any of the liabilities of the Partnership incurred thereafter; provided, however, such Partner shall be entitled to receive a pro rata or other agreed share of any royalties earned from the exploitation of any phonorecord recorded hereunder and embodying his performances as and when such royalties are actually received by the Partnership, less his pro rata or other agreed share of any expenses. It is hereby agreed by the Partners that for the purposes of determining the net worth of a disassociating Partner, the Group Name shall be valued, except as provided herein, at One Dollar ($1.00).

(b) The net worth of the Partnership shall be determined as of the date of disassociation by an accountant selected by the remaining Partners other than the Partnership's regular accountant, and other than the personal accountant of any Partner, and such accountant shall be familiar with the music industry. The accountant shall make said determination in accordance with generally accepted accounting practices and principles, taking into consideration, among other factors, the fair market value of the assets of the Partnership (other than the Group Name), its liabilities (including the disassociated Partner's entitlement to future record royalties as provided in Subclause (a) above), its past profits, and losses. If the disassociated Partner or his legal representative should disagree with the accountant's determination in the event of disassociation for any other reason, the disassociated Partner or such representative may within thirty (30) days after receipt of the accountant's determination submit the issue of the fair market value of the Partnership to arbitration, under the applicable rules of the American Arbitration Association. Unless the remaining Partner(s) elect to pay the disassociated Partner's share of the value of the Partnership sooner, said share (including interest on the unpaid balance at the prime rate per annum accruing from said date of final determination) shall be payable in 60 equal monthly installments commencing one month following the date of the final determination of said net worth.

16. PARTNER WITHDRAWAL:

If a Partner retires or is caused to involuntarily leave the Partnership as a result of breaching this agreement, he shall be entitled to the same compensation as a disassociated partner less the damage his departure has caused the Partnership. As with the value of the Partnership, the damage to the Partnership will be determined by an independent accountant selected by the remaining Partners. The withdrawing Partner has no rights to challenge the determinations of the accountant chosen by the remaining Partners.

17. RIGHTS TO GROUP NAME:

Upon disassociation or withdrawal, either voluntarily or otherwise, of Partner A from the Partnership, the Partnership shall no longer operate in any manner under the Group Name, unless otherwise agreed to by departing Partner A or his legal representative, such permission not to be unreasonably withheld. Similarly, upon dissolution of the Partnership, the Partnership shall no longer operate in any manner under the Group Name. Should Partner A form a new band with two or more Partners of the Band, this new band may use the Group Name without any compensation to the Partnership or the other members. Provided this new band actively performs with each of said partners substantive involvement for at least three years, the new band may continue to use the Group Name in accordance with whatever agreement is entered into by that band's members. Other partners may not operate under the Group Name or derivations thereof, whether confusingly similar or not.

18. DISSOLUTION:

(a) This Agreement shall terminate and the Partnership shall be dissolved, upon the first to occur of the following events:

(i) The written agreement of all of the Partners to dissolve the Partnership; or

(ii) By operation of law, except as otherwise provided herein.

(b) The addition of a new Partner (as provided in Clause 14 hereof), the disassociation of a Partner (as provided in Clause 15 hereof), or the withdrawal of a Partner (as provided in Clause 16 hereof) shall not terminate the Agreement, and it shall remain in full force and effect among the remaining Partners.

(c) Upon termination of the Partnership, the Partnership's receivables shall be collected and its assets liquidated forthwith (except as provided in Subclauses (e) and (f) below). The proceeds from the liquidation of the Partnership assets and collection of the Partnership receivables shall be applied in the following order:

(i) First, to the expense of liquidation and debts of the Partnership other than debts owing to any of the Partners;

(ii) Next, to the debts owing to any of the Partners, including debts arising from loans made to or for the benefit of the Partnership, except that if the amount of such proceeds is insufficient to pay such debts in full, payment shall be made on a pro rata basis;

(iii) Next, in payment to each Partner of any financial capital investment made by him in the Partnership belonging to him, except that if the amount of such proceeds is insufficient to pay such financial capital investment in full, payment shall be made on a pro rata basis;

(iv) Next, in payment to each Partner or a pro rata basis of any of such proceeds remaining.

(d) The Partners shall execute all such instruments for facilitating the collection of the Partnership receivables and liquidation of the Partnership assets, and for the mutual indemnity or release of the Partners as may be appropriate.

(e) Any property, including, but not limited to, all rights and interest in contracts, agreements, options, choices in actions and Merchandising Rights owned or controlled by the Partnership at the time of dissolution from which income is being derived shall not be sold, but shall be assigned to Partner E or a company controlled by Partner E. Partner E agrees to administer those contracts and to distribute proceeds therefrom on an annual basis in accordance with the provisions Subclause 18(c) above. Partner E shall maintain and keep for a period of at least three (3) years, complete and accurate records in accordance with generally accepted accounting principles in sufficient detail to enable appropriate revenues, costs and payments to be determined. Upon the request of another Partner, but not exceeding once in any year, Partner E shall permit an independent public accountant, to have access to all such records necessary to verify the accuracy of payments. Any such audit shall be at the expense of Partners requesting the audit, except that if any such inspection reveals a deficiency in payments of ten percent (10%) or more, then the expense of such audit plus any shortfall amounts shall be borne promptly by Partner E. If such audit reveals a surplus in payments actually paid, the Partners shall refund to Partner E the surplus amount within thirty (30) days after such audit.

19. ACCOUNTING:

(a) Fiscal Year:

The fiscal year of the Partnership shall be determined by the Partners after consultation with the Partnership's accountants.

(b) Accounting Method:

The Partnership books shall be kept on a cash basis.

(c) Determination of Profit and Loss:

The Partnership shall render yearly accounting to each Partner on the 30th day of [INSERT MONTH] and every year during the term of the Partnership.

20. BOOKS AND RECORDS:

Proper and complete books of account of the Partnership business shall be kept at the Partnership's principal place of business and shall be open to inspection by the Partners or their accredited representatives at any reasonable time during normal business hours.

21. PARTNERSHIP BANK ACCOUNTS:

One or more Partnership bank accounts may be opened and maintained by the Partners with such bank or banks as the Partners may determine and any checks or withdrawals from or against any bank account or accounts shall be upon the signature of Partner D; provided, however, that such checks or withdrawals shall be subject to the approval process set out in Clause 8 hereinabove.

22. ASSIGNMENT OF PARTNER'S INTEREST:

No Partner, or executor, or administrator of a deceased Partner shall sell, assign, or transfer all or any portion of his financial or other interest in the Partnership or right to receive a share of Partnership assets, profits or other distributions without the prior written consent of all of the other Partners and any such purported sale, assignment, or transfer in contravention of the foregoing shall be null and void. The Partners acknowledge that a part of the capital contribution of each Partner is the unique personal services required to be rendered on the exclusive account of the Partnership by each Partner, for which no presently adequate substitute exists; and that the other Partners are the sole and exclusive judges of the adequacy of any future substitution.

23. MISCELLANEOUS:

(a) Indemnity:

Each Partner hereby indemnifies the other Partner(s) and holds such other Partner(s) harmless against and from all claims, demands, actions, and rights of action which shall or may arise by virtue of anything done or admitted to be done by him (through or by agents, employees or other representatives) outside the scope of or in breach of the terms of this Agreement. Each Partner shall promptly notify the other Partner(s) if such Partner knows the existence of a claim, demand, action, or right of action.

(b) Successors and Assigns:

Subject to the restrictions on assignments set forth in this Agreement, the provisions of this Agreement shall be binding upon and inure to the benefit of the heirs, executors, administrators, successors, and assigns of the Partnership.

(c) Severability:

If any term, provision, covenant, or condition of this Agreement is held to be illegal or invalid for any reason whatsoever, such illegality or invalidity shall not affect the validity of the remainder of this Agreement.

(d) Gender:

Wherever required in this Agreement, the singular shall include the plural, and the masculine gender shall include the feminine and the neuter.

24. CONSTRUCTION:

This Agreement shall be governed by and construed in accordance with the laws of the State of [_____] applicable to contracts entered into and fully to be performed in [_____]. In the event of any action, arbitration, suit, or proceeding arising from or under this Agreement, the prevailing party shall be entitled to recover reasonable attorneys' fees and costs of said action, suit, arbitration, or proceeding. This is the entire understanding of the Partners relating to the subject matter hereof and supersedes all prior and collateral agreements, understandings, and negotiations of the parties. Each Partner acknowledges that no representation, inducements, promises, understandings or agreements, oral or written, with reference to the subject matter hereof have been made other than as expressly set forth herein. Each Partner acknowledges that he has consulted with legal counsel of his choice with respect to the contents of this Agreement prior to execution hereof, and has been advised by such counsel with respect to the meaning and consequences hereof. This Agreement cannot be changed, rescinded, or terminated except by a writing signed by each of the Partners. The titles of the clauses of this Agreement are for convenience only, and shall not in any way affect the interpretation of any clauses of this Agreement or of the Agreement itself.

IN WITNESS WHEREOF, the parties have executed this Agreement as of the day and year first above written.

"PARTNERS"

_____

_____

_____

_____

_____

_____

Appendix B

COPYRIGHT SPLIT AGREEMENT

This Copyright Split Agreement, (this "Agreement") entered into as of _____, by and among the following persons (all of whom are collectively referred to herein as the "Writers"):

Singer   215 S. Aretha Avenue
                                Chicago, Illinois 60654

Guitarist   2000 6th Street
                                Chicago, IL 60654

Bassist   1150 Mt. Bootsy Court
                                Chicago, IL 60654

Drummer   372 W. St. Zigaboo Road
                                Chicago, IL 60654

The Writers do hereby acknowledge and agree as follows:

1. COPYRIGHT OWNERSHIP. The Writers have collaborated in the creation of the musical composition set forth below ("Composition") and the Writers shall be deemed to be the authors of the Composition pursuant to and in accordance with the applicable copyright ownership percentages set forth below ("Applicable Percentages"). Accordingly, the Writers each agree to list the Writers as the authors of the Composition in the Applicable Percentages on any and all documents relating to the Composition, including, without limitation, copyright registration forms and information that may be provided to music publishers and performing rights societies.

    1.1 Name of Artist Performing Composition: Band

    1.2 Name of Composition: _____

    1.3 Record Number: _____

Applicable Percentages:

Singer	_____%	Guitarist	_____%
Bassist	_____%	Drummer	_____%

2. PUBLISHING. Each of the Writers shall have the right to administer such Writer's Applicable Percentage of the Composition without any restriction.

3. GOVERNING LAW; CHOICE OF VENUE. THIS AGREEMENT IS GOVERNED BY AND SHALL BE CONSTRUED IN ACCORDANCE WITH THE LAW OF THE STATE OF ILLINOIS, EXCLUDING ANY CONFLICT-OF-LAWS RULE OR PRINCIPLE THAT MIGHT REFER THE GOVERNANCE OR THE CONSTRUCTION OF THIS AGREEMENT TO THE LAW OF ANOTHER JURISDICTION. In the event of any dispute between the parties, such dispute shall be brought in the state and federal courts sitting in Cook County in the state of Illinois.

4. FURTHER ASSURANCES. In connection with this Agreement and the transactions contemplated hereby, each Writer shall execute and deliver any additional documents and instruments and perform any additional acts that may be necessary or appropriate to effectuate and perform the provisions of this Agreement and those transactions.

* * * * * *

IN WITNESS WHEREOF, the Writers have executed this Agreement as of the date first set forth above.

Writers:

_____
Singer

_____
Guitarist

_____
Bassist

_____
Drummer

Appendix C

COPYRIGHT ASSIGNMENT

THIS COPYRIGHT ASSIGNMENT (this "Assignment") is made and entered into as of [DATE] ("Effective Date") by and between [SINGER, GUITARIST, BASSIST, and DRUMMER] ("Assignors"), and [BAND/BAND ADDRESS] ("Assignee").

Singer   215 S. Aretha Avenue
                                            Chicago, IL 60654

Guitarist   2000 6th Street
                                            Chicago, IL 60654

Bassist   1150 Mt. Bootsy Court
                                            Chicago, IL 60654

Drummer   372 W. St. Zigaboo Road
                                            Chicago, IL 60654

WHEREAS, Assignors have collaborated in the creation of the musical compositions and sound recordings set forth in Exhibit A ("Works"). Assignors wish to assign to Assignee, and Assignee wishes to acquire from Assignors, all right, title and interest in the Works.

NOW, THEREFORE, for good and valuable consideration, the receipt and sufficiency of which are hereby acknowledged:

1. Assignors hereby sell, assign, transfer and set over to Assignee the entire right, title and interest in and to any and all intellectual property associated with the Works, including Copyrights for the United States and all foreign countries, including, without limitation, any registrations and applications therefore, any renewals and extensions of the registrations, all of the exclusive rights listed in 17 U.S.C. § 106 and all other corresponding rights that are or may be secured under the laws of the United States or any foreign country, now or hereafter in effect, together with all physical or tangible embodiments of the Works, in Assignors' possession or under Assignors' control, for Assignee's own use and enjoyment, and for the use and enjoyment of Assignee's

successors, assigns or other legal representatives, as fully and entirely as the same would have been held and enjoyed by Assignors if this Assignment had not been made.

2. Assignors hereby authorize and request the Register of Copyrights of the United States, and the corresponding entity or agency in any applicable foreign country, to record Assignee as the assignee and owner of the Works.

3. Each Assignor represents and warrants that: (i) it is the sole and exclusive owner of the entire right, title and interest in and to its contributions to the Works (including the corresponding rights set forth above) free and clear of any liens, security interests or other encumbrances; (ii) it has the full right and authority to execute this Assignment and to assign to Assignee the rights assigned herein; and (iii) it has not executed, and will not execute any agreement or other instrument in conflict herewith.

4. Assignors shall take all further actions, and provide to Assignee, Assignee's successors, assigns or other legal representatives, all such cooperation and assistance (including, without limitation, the execution and delivery of any and all affidavits, declarations, oaths, exhibits, assignments, powers of attorney or other documentation) requested by Assignee to more fully and effectively effectuate the purpose of this Assignment, including, without limitation with respect to: (1) the preparation and prosecution of any applications for registration, or any applications for renewal, relating to the rights assigned herein; (2) the prosecution or defense of any Copyright Office proceeding, infringement, or other proceedings that may arise in connection with any of the rights assigned herein, including, without limitation, testifying as to any facts relating to the Works or this Assignment; (3) obtaining any additional copyright protection relating to the rights assigned herein that Assignee may deem appropriate which may be secured under the laws now or hereafter in effect in the United States or any other country; and (4) the implementation or perfection of this Assignment in all applicable jurisdictions throughout the world.

5. Assignors agree that Assignee shall have the right to use and permit others to use Assignors' names, voices, likenesses and other biographical information in connection with the exploitation of the Works.

* * * * *

IN WITNESS WHEREOF, Assignors and Assignee have caused this Assignment to be executed by their duly authorized representatives as of the Effective Date.

ASSIGNORS   **ASSIGNEE**

_____   _____
Singer

_____   Name:_____
Guitarist

_____   Title:_____
Bassist

_____
Drummer

Notary

STATE OF   )
)
COUNTRY OF   )

On this ____ day of _____, there appeared before me _____, personally known to me, who acknowledged that he signed the foregoing Assignment as his voluntary act and deed on behalf and with full authority of _____.

                                            _____
                                            Notary Public

Appendix D

WORK-MADE-FOR-HIRE AGREEMENT

THIS WORK-MADE-FOR-HIRE AGREEMENT (this "Agreement") is made and entered into as of [DATE] ("Effective Date") by and between [BAND MEMBER], an individual, living at _____ ("Band Member"), and [BAND/BAND ADDRESS] ("Band").

1. Band hereby engages Band Member's services and Band Member hereby accepts such engagement to perform musical services, including, without limitation, songwriting, performing and recording, in connection with all musical compositions and sound recordings created by and for Band, from the Effective Date until the termination of this engagement ("Works").

2. Band shall pay Band Member _____ as full and complete consideration for Band Member's services associated with this Agreement.

3. Band Member agrees that all of its services pursuant to this Agreement shall be considered works-made-for-hire as defined in 17 U.S.C § 101, and as such, Band shall own the entire right, title and interest in and to any and all intellectual property associated with Band Member's contributions to the Works, including Copyrights for the United States and all foreign countries, including, without limitation, any registrations and applications therefore, any renewals and extensions of the registrations, all of the exclusive rights listed in 17 U.S.C. § 106 and all other corresponding rights that are or may be secured under the laws of the United States or any foreign country.

4. Band Member agrees that Band shall have the right to use and permit others to use Band Member's name, voice, likeness and other biographical information in connection with the exploitation of the Works.

5. The engagement set forth in this Agreement shall be effective as of the Effective Date until termination by either Band Member or Band. No termination of this agreement will be binding unless confirmed in writing and signed by Band Member and Band. Band Member acknowledges that termination of this Agreement will not affect the ownership of the Works and that Band will remain the sole and rightful owner of the Works.

6. In the event that Band Member's contributions are not found to be valid works-made-for-hire, Band Member hereby sells, assigns, transfers and sets over to Band its entire right, title and interest in and to any and all intellectual property associated with the Works, including Copyrights for the United States

and all foreign countries, including, without limitation, any registrations and applications therefore, any renewals and extensions of the registrations, all of the exclusive rights listed in 17 U.S.C. § 106 and all other corresponding rights that are or may be secured under the laws of the United States or any foreign country, now or hereafter in effect, together with all physical or tangible embodiments of the Works, in Band Member's possession or under Band Member's control, for Band's own use and enjoyment, and for the use and enjoyment of Band's successors, assigns or other legal representatives, as fully and entirely as the same would have been held and enjoyed by Band Member if the assignment under this Agreement had not been made.

7. In the event that Band Member's contributions are not found to be valid works-made-for-hire, Band Member hereby authorizes and requests the Register of Copyrights of the United States, and the corresponding entity or agency in any applicable foreign country, to record Band as the assignee and owner of the Works.

8. Band Member represents and warrants that: (i) it has contributed to the Works and has not assigned any right, title or interest in its contributions to the Works but for this Agreement; (ii) it has the full right and authority to execute this Agreement and to assign to Band any rights assigned herein; and (iii) it has not executed, and will not execute any agreement or other instrument in conflict herewith.

9. Band Member shall take all further actions, and provide to Band, Band's successors, assigns or other legal representatives, all such cooperation and assistance (including, without limitation, the execution and delivery of any and all affidavits, declarations, oaths, exhibits, assignments, powers of attorney or other documentation) requested by Band to more fully and effectively effectuate the purpose of this Agreement, including, without limitation with respect to: (1) the preparation and prosecution of any applications for registration, or any applications for renewal, relating to any rights assigned herein; (2) the prosecution or defense of any Copyright Office proceeding, infringement, or other proceedings that may arise in connection with any rights assigned herein, including, without limitation, testifying as to any facts relating to the Works or this Agreement; (3) obtaining any additional copyright protection relating to any rights assigned herein that Band may deem appropriate which may be secured under the laws now or hereafter in effect in the United States or any other country; and (4) the implementation or perfection of this Agreement in all applicable jurisdictions throughout the world.

* * * * *

IN WITNESS WHEREOF, Band Member and Band have caused this Agreement to be executed by their duly authorized representatives as of the Effective Date.

BAND MEMBER   BAND

_____   _____

Band Member   Name:_____

                                     Title:_____

Appendix E

COVER ART ASSIGNMENT

THIS COVER ART ASSIGNMENT (this "Assignment") is made and entered into as of [DATE] ("Effective Date") by and between [ARTIST/PHOTOGRA-PHER], an individual, living at _____ ("Assignor"), and [BAND/BAND ADDRESS] ("Assignee").

WHEREAS, in exchange for $[DOLLAR AMOUNT], receipt of which is acknowledged, Assignor wishes to assign to Assignee, and Assignee wishes to acquire from Assignor, all right, title and interest in the creative works depicted in Exhibit A, and all works substantially similar thereto created by the Assignor ("Works").

NOW, THEREFORE, for good and valuable consideration, the receipt and sufficiency of which are hereby acknowledged, Assignor hereby sells, assigns, transfers and sets over to Assignee the entire right, title and interest in and to any and all intellectual property associated with the Works, including Copyrights for the United States and all foreign countries, including, without limitation, any registrations and applications therefore, any renewals and extensions of the registrations, all of the exclusive rights listed in 17 U.S.C. § 106 and all other corresponding rights that are or may be secured under the laws of the United States or any foreign country, now or hereafter in effect, together with all physical or tangible embodiments of the Works, in Assignor's possession or under Assignor's control, for Assignee's own use and enjoyment, and for the use and enjoyment of Assignee's successors, assigns or other legal representatives, as fully and entirely as the same would have been held and enjoyed by Assignor if this Assignment had not been made.

Assignor hereby authorizes and requests the Register of Copyrights of the United States, and the corresponding entity or agency in any applicable foreign country, to record Assignee as the assignee and owner of the Works.

Assignor represents and warrants that: (i) it is the sole and exclusive owner of the entire right, title and interest in and to the Works (including the corresponding rights set forth above), free and clear of any liens, security interests or other encumbrances; (ii) it has the full right and authority to execute this Assignment and to assign to Assignee the rights assigned herein; and (iii) it has not executed, and will not, execute any agreement or other instrument in conflict herewith.

Assignor shall take all further actions, and provide to Assignee, Assignee's successors, assigns or other legal representatives, all such cooperation and assistance (including, without limitation, the execution and delivery of any and all affidavits, declarations, oaths, exhibits, assignments, powers of attorney or other documentation) requested by Assignee to more fully and effectively effectuate the purpose of this Assignment, including, without limitation with respect to: (1) the preparation and prosecution of any applications for registration, or any applications for renewal, relating to the rights assigned herein; (2) the prosecution or defense of any Copyright Office proceeding, infringement, or other proceedings that may arise in connection with any of the rights assigned herein, including, without limitation, testifying as to any facts relating to the Works or this Assignment; (3) obtaining any additional copyright protection relating to the rights assigned herein that Assignee may deem appropriate which may be secured under the laws now or hereafter in effect in the United States or any other country; and (4) the implementation or perfection of this Assignment in all applicable jurisdictions throughout the world.

Assignor is granted a royalty-free license to use the work to market and promote his services.

*   *   *   *   *

IN WITNESS WHEREOF, Assignor and Assignee have caused this Assignment to be executed by their duly authorized representatives as of the Effective Date.

[ARTIST/PHOTOGRAPHER NAME]   [BAND]

_____   _____

Name:_____   Name:_____

Title:_____   Title:_____

Notary

STATE OF   )
)
COUNTRY OF   )

On this ____ day of _____, there appeared before me _____, personally known to me, who acknowledged that he signed the foregoing Assignment as his voluntary act and deed on behalf and with full authority of _____.

_____
Notary Public

About the Authors

Barry Irwin is the founding member of Irwin IP LLC. Since 1992, he has primarily practiced in the area of intellectual property litigation, first-chairing many high-stakes matters. He has served as a member of Lawyers for the Creative Art's Board since 2010. Barry has also been legal counsel to numerous bands and musicians, addressing music law related issues ranging from drafting partnership agreements, preparing copyright filings, negotiating recording contracts, litigating termination of recording contracts, and winding up band assets upon dissolution. Barry received his B.S. in Aerospace Engineering in 1988, and his J.D, *magna cum laude,* in 1992 from the University of Notre Dame. Barry is also an Adjunct Professor at Notre Dame Law School, where he teaches Patent Litigation and Advanced Copyright Concepts.

Adam Reis is an associate at Irwin IP LLC where he focuses on intellectual property litigation and entertainment law. He represents bands and performing artists in a wide range of matters and across several genres of music. Adam received his B.A. in Chemistry from Miami University in 2010 and his J.D. from Chicago-Kent College of Law in 2015.

The authors would like to thank Chris DeLillo, Alyssa Cantor, Dan Sito, and Nick Fuller for their valuable research and writing assistance in putting this book together.